Secrets of the Prophets

Secrets of the Prophets

Dale Spears

CFI
Springville, Utah

ISBN 13: 978-1-59955-283-5

Published by CFI, an imprint of Cedar Fort, Inc., 2373 W. 700 S., Springville, UT 84663
Distributed by Cedar Fort, Inc., www.cedarfort.com

LIBRARY OF CONGRESS CATALOGING-IN-PUBLICATION DATA

Spears, Dale.
Secrets of the prophets / Dale Spears.
p. cm.
ISBN 978-1-59955-283-5 (acid-free paper)
1. Prophets (Mormon theology) 2. Religion and science--History. 3. Church of Jesus Christ of Latter-day Saints--Doctrines. 4. Mormon Church--Doctrines. I. Title.

BX8643.P7S64 2009
231.7'45--dc22

2009009794

Cover design by Nicole Williams
Cover design © 2009 by Lyle Mortimer
Edited and typeset by Heidi Doxey

Printed in the United States of America

10 9 8 7 6 5 4 3 2 1

Printed on acid-free paper

Table of Contents

Part I

Prophets Know Science

From the early history of the world, there have been men who have known things that others have not known. These men are called prophets. They tell us the reason they know these mysterious things is that God tells them. They are in direct contact with God and can find out things from him that cannot be known in any other way. Of course, prophets have never been listened to very well. They tell the people what God says and the people usually go ahead and do just what they want to do anyway.

Today we seem to rely more on physical scientists to tell us about the world and how it works, and on social scientists to tell us what we should be doing. We have wonderful technology that allows us to travel all over the world in a matter of days. We have medicine that cures many diseases. We have labor-saving devices that make life easier for us. We have computers and technology that are just jaw dropping to the older generations. Science has done much for us.

Of course, technology is also causing pollution which increases global warming and may eventually overheat the earth and kill all life on it. Our travel through the world is spreading plant and animal pests wherever we go. Our medicines cure diseases, but many germs are becoming resistant to them so we may have pandemic diseases coming. The Internet is wonderful but its number one use has become to view pornography. Science is good only if it is used correctly, but we seem to have trouble with that.

Do you think that perhaps prophets could help us with our science so we need not make so many mistakes? If they get their information from God then they should be able to tell us many things that will help us. Let us look at some of the things that prophets have told us and see how scientific discoveries and prophetic revelations fit together.

1

Plate Tectonics in Prophecy—Standing on Infirm Ground

If you look at a map of the globe you may notice that the outlines of the continents fit together somewhat like a jigsaw puzzle. Sometime around 1912, Alfred Wegener noticed this and came up with the theory that the continents, at some point in the past, were all one land and that this land had broken apart into continents. He postulated that the continents had moved to spread over the earth to where they are now. He called this big single continent Pangaea, meaning "all lands." Other scientists rejected this hypothesis, replying that the earth was firm, solid, immovable and that it always had been.

Wegener looked for something to back up his theory. He noticed that the fossils were the same on the west coast of Africa and the east coast of South America. According to his theory, these two places would have been joined at one time. The fossils were also the same in Europe and North America where his theory said they were once joined and on the coasts of India and Madagascar. This seemed to indicate that these places had all once been connected together. The other scientists were still not convinced.

Next, Wegener said that the moving of continents would cause mountains. As the continents moved, they crashed together and this caused mountains to be pushed up. The other scientists said, no, the earth is cooling and shrinking and this is what causes mountains.

Arthur Holmes tried to help with the theory of thermal convection. The theory of thermal convection says that the mantle on the inside of the earth is liquid (as volcanoes show when liquid rock comes out of them) and that there are currents in this liquid rock, just as there are currents in the ocean. When the currents move about, they push on the continents and move them. Seismic readings, however, indicated that the center of the earth was solid, not liquid. Thermal convection seemed just another theory with no proof. Mr. Wegener worked on his theory of continental movement until his death in 1930 but could not convince the other scientists that he knew what he was talking about.

It wasn't until the 1960s that scientists discovered mid-ocean ridges and their geomagnetic anomalies. This, along with island arcs being found next to ocean trenches, caused the idea of continental drift to be revisited. With these discoveries, there was enough evidence to show that Wegener might be right. Now, at last, scientists have come around to his way of thinking. Pangaea, the super continent, and its breakup are now accepted in scientific circles.[1]

What does this have to do with religion? For one thing, it shows that what took scientists so long to figure out should have already been known to readers of the Bible. If they had read the Bible, they would have noticed a little verse in the book of Genesis that says, "In [Peleg's] days was the earth divided" (Genesis 10:25). Before modern times, people interpreted this to mean that the earth was divided among the different peoples, but the idea of Pangaea being divided was in the Bible all along. The scientists just had to collect their own evidence before they would believe it.

Also, if we look at a revelation given to the Prophet Joseph Smith in the year 1831 we read: "He [God] shall command the great deep [the ocean], and it shall be driven back into the north countries, and the islands [continents] shall become one land; And the land of Jerusalem and the land of Zion shall be turned back into their own place, and the earth shall be like as it was in the days before it was divided" (D&C 133:23–24). The Book of Mormon calls the American Continent an isle of the sea (see 2 Nephi 10:20). The continents are all surrounded by water, and since they broke off from Pangaea they could be called islands. Nephi also says the great deep will be driven back to the north so the land will go to the south. This agrees with Wegener's thought that Pangaea was located near the South Pole.

Thus we see the prophets were a good bit ahead of the scientists. The book of Genesis has been around 4,000 years and recorded the original separation. Joseph Smith lived in the 1800s. Both accounts tell us that the continents had once been one land, but few people listened. It wasn't until the 1960s that scientists finally confirmed what Joseph Smith and the prophets who wrote the Bible already knew. Science has finally come to support religion with regard to continental drift.

It should be noted that according to the Bible, the earth was divided about two hundred years after the flood. This would be about 2,200 BC, or around 4,000 years ago. Wegener thought it was about 30 million years ago that Pangaea broke up into the continents. Now, if you ask geologists and ecologists, they will tell you that the rate of erosion on the earth is such that the highest mountains in existence would all be broken up and washed into the sea in about 20 million years. This means that no fossils can be more than 20 million years old since they would have all been destroyed in the erosion process. Thus the fossils Wegener used to connect the continents could not be more than 20 million years old. Scientists have not noticed this disparity yet, but give them time. They are smart fellows and in time they will catch up with what the prophets have told us.

Notes:

1. "Plate Tectonics: The Rocky History of an Idea," University of California Museum of Paleontology, http://www.ucmp.berkeley.edu/geology/techist.html

2

Fiber Optics in Prophecy—I Saw the Light

There is a new technology beginning to be rather widely used that is called "fiber optics." Some time ago, near Christmas time, my niece brought in a fiber optic Christmas tree. It was somewhat like a regular Christmas tree, but it had little filaments or small glass rods mixed in with the branches. Each one of these glass rods had a tiny spark of light at the end of it. A small turning filter caused the light to change color as the filter turned. It was a very beautiful sparkling tree. I decided to buy one. I joined the fiber optic age.

Pretty light shows are just one use of fiber optics. A more useful application of fiber optics is in communication. If you replace telephone lines with fiber optic cables, you find that the fiber optics are smaller and lighter, so they are easier to install than metal telephone cables. Also the signals move faster through the glass fibers than through metal cables. You can also send more information through. Pulses of light do not interfere with other light pulses, which means you can have messages going both ways in the cable at the same time. In metal cables the electricity can only go one way at a time. For all of these reasons, fiber optics are quickly replacing telephone cables.[1]

Now let us see what this has to do with religion. In Revelation 4:6 we read, "And before the throne [of God] there was a sea of glass, like unto crystal." Then in Revelation 15:2, "And I saw as it were a sea of glass mingled with fire [light?]: and them that had gotten the victory . . . stand on the sea of glass, having the harps of God." Here we have before the throne of God a sea of glass like unto crystal where the saved of God who have the victory over evil and death stand. They are not floating on clouds like the old tradition goes.

Where would a sea of glass or crystal come from? We are told that the wicked will be burned at the coming of the Lord and that the elements will melt with fervent heat (see 2 Peter 3:10; D&C 101:25). If great heat were applied to the earth what would happen to it? If sand is heated—and sand covers much of the earth—it makes glass. If the earth were heated until the sand and rocks of the earth melted, then what would be left would be a like unto a sea of glass. Could this be what the revelation is talking about?

Now the Prophet Joseph says, speaking of the angels, "They reside in the presence of God, on a globe (planet) like a sea of glass and fire, where all things for their glory are manifest. . . . This earth, in its sanctified and immortal state, will be made like unto crystal and will be a Urim and Thummim to the inhabitants who dwell thereon, whereby all things . . . will be manifest to those who dwell on it" (D&C 130:7–9).

The Urim and Thummim is an instrument with which the Lord's people can learn the things of God (see Numbers 27:21). It is like a telephone to the spiritual realm. The Prophet Joseph says the earth will become a Urim and Thummim to the saved people who dwell on it. Thus we see that the Prophet Joseph knew of fiber optics before it was invented. By looking in the glass or stone or crystal we have a way to get information that is exactly the same as fiber optics. Just as a TV screen looks a lot like a stone, is made of glass, and pictures come through it, so also will we be able to see things in the crystal earth. Of course there were no televisions when John wrote the Book of Revelation, nor when Joseph Smith wrote what he did about the earth becoming a Urim and Thummim back in 1843. The prophets knew about fiber optics, or something very similar, long before they were invented, but men are now catching up with the prophets—at least in some things.

Notes:

1. "Optical Fiber," Wikipedia, http://en.wikipedia.org/wiki/Optical_fiber

3

Global Dimming in Prophecy—The Benefits of Pollution

In the Old Testament, we are told by the prophet Joel that in the days before the second coming there would be darkness on the earth. He said, "The sun and the moon shall be darkened, and the stars shall withdraw their shining" (Joel 3:15; see also Matthew 24:29 and Mark 13:24). Now I don't think that anything is going to happen to the sun, but there is another way that the light of heaven can be darkened—by air pollution. The sun and moon will not go out but they will be harder to see. If there is enough air pollution, then the stars may not be seen at all. Is this happening?

In the 1960s, Dr. Gerald Stanhill, of the Israel Ministry of Agriculture, began observing how much sunlight reached the earth. This information was used in Israel to judge how to irrigate and raise crops. In the 1980s he repeated the experiment to see if there was a difference, and if they needed to change how farmers worked with their crops. He found that there was a 22 percent drop in the amount of sunlight reaching the earth in the nation of Israel. Something was blocking the sunlight from reaching the earth.[1]

Beate Liepert of Germany found the same thing in his country. He started looking in weather journals to see if this was happening anywhere else. Between the 1950s and 1990s, the level of solar energy reaching the earth had dropped 9 percent in Antarctica, 10 percent in areas of the U.S.A., almost 30 percent in one region of Russia, and 16 percent in parts of the British Isles. Wherever it was measured, the sun had become darkened by 9 percent to 30 percent. He called this "global dimming." The sun was being darkened.[2]

Perhaps I should mention here that other scientists ignored his research for a time because they were that if global dimming was going on they could not simultaneously have global warming. Later work showed that global dimming was actually slowing global warming and that without it, the earth would be getting hotter much faster.

David Travis, a scientist, was studying the effect of vapor trails left by high-flying airplanes on the weather. The problem was that the vapor trails were always in the air. How could he know what change they caused if they were always there? Then on September 12, 2001, because of what happened in the destruction of the World Trade Center, almost all flights were cancelled for three days. During this time he measured the average temperature range and found the temperature nation-wide went up over two degrees Fahrenheit. Airplane vapor trails were making a real difference.[3]

There is less sunlight reaching the earth, but the earth's temperature is going up. Global dimming has helped slow down global warming, but has not stopped it. To stop global warming, we may need to put more pollutants in the air that reflect the sun light. Doing this we may be able to cool the earth back down and avoid a runaway greenhouse effect. The sun has already been darkened, but we may have to darken it more to bring down the earth's temperature. If the earth is sick and has a temperature we need to do something to cure it. The darkening of the sun may help.

Thus we see that in our time the sun and the moon has been darkened and the prophets have been justified in their prophecies. Only time will tell how much darker it will get.

Notes:

1. "Dimming the Sun," *Nova*, April 18, 2006. (Available online at: http://www.pbs.org/wgbh/nova/transcripts/3310_sun.html).
2. Ibid.
3. Ibid.

4

Creating Life—According to Prophets vs. Up from the Ooze

In the year 1953, Stanley Miller conducted a number of experiments in which he tried to create life from nonliving things. He put the chemicals that were thought to exist in the early atmosphere and oceans of the earth in a test tube in order to recreate the conditions that were on Earth when evolutionary scientists believe life began. He added a little electricity to take the place of lightning. He soon found a few amino acids in the mixture, but little else. He changed the mixture, and was successful in creating the building blocks of life but unsuccessful in creating life itself.[1]

These experiments were done according to the theory of evolution, trying to show that life can come from nonlife. Of course life can come from nonliving things. All living organisms now on the earth were once not alive. All it takes is some spark to begin the process. If God is alive, then he could begin the process of making life from nonliving elements. Perhaps this is why God is often called in the scriptures "the living God." Now let us take a broader look at the process to see what we can conclude from it.

After he had so little success with the first experiments, Miller changed the formula in order to increase his chances for success. Did the earth change its formula when it did not have life at the beginning? Was the earth deciding to create life and looking for the right formula to make it happen as Miller did? Probably not. God may possess the intelligence to do that, but nonliving elements do not.

The main thing we notice is that Miller's experiment was conducted by human intelligence. Stanley Miller used his intelligence to put together the apparatus and to decide what chemicals to include in the mixture. He reasoned that he could use electricity to replace lightning. Thus, there would not have been a spontaneous creation of life, even if life had been created in his experiment. If he had succeeded, critics could have said that an intelligent creator was not needed to create life. He did not succeed, therefore we can say that a more intelligent being than Stanley Miller is needed in order to create life, unless he does it God's way and becomes a father. He did nothing more than show that intelligence is needed to create life.

To find life being created on its own, just observe what is happening in nature. The land and oceans have a great deal more of the chemicals of life than they had when life was supposed to have appeared. Why aren't scientists watching to see if new kinds of life are coming into existence? They do not seem to want to consider this possibility. They say life happened only once and may never happen again. If evolution is true, life should be appearing all the time in the very thick organic soup that makes up the oceans now. Could it be that they have so little faith in evolution that they do not believe it can happen now without human help? It seems that way.

If life can't be made now without intelligent human help, how could it have been made in the beginning without intelligent help? This is a contradiction. There were no people on Earth then. Could it be that even scientists, somewhere deep in their hearts, believe that life began with the help of God or at least some outside source of intelligence? They certainly act that way. If the intelligence of men is needed to create life now, then God was needed to create life then. Perhaps some scientists are moving closer to believing in God than we think or they admit.

One of the rules scientists have is that life comes only from other life. Yet in the theory of evolution they say that life came from nonliving things. This is a contradiction. They say when the conditions are right, life will automatically appear, yet with conditions now a great deal better than when life supposedly appeared the first time, they say no life is forthcoming unless men make it happen. This does not make sense. It makes more sense to say that God created life by taking spirits that were already with him and putting them into bodies created for the purpose.

Notes

1. William D. Stansfield, *The Science of Evolution,* (New York: Macmillan Publishing Company, 1977), 52–53.

5

Genetics in Prophecy— Each after Its Own Kind

Gregor Mendel was an Austrian monk and later an abbot. He read about Charles Darwin's theory of evolution and did not like the idea very much. He decided to try to do something about it. Mendel wanted to show that evolutionary change could come from crossbreeding, and he thought this would be a strike against Darwin's evolution.

In the year 1856 Mendel began a series of experiments with pea plants. He crossbred plants with different characteristics: tall pea plants with short pea plants, yellow-hulled peas with green-hulled, wrinkled peas with smooth, and so forth. He kept very careful track of what happened to the descendants of the original pea plants. From this, he formulated laws of heredity that are still in use today. Unfortunately for him, he did not prove his idea that crossbreeding has caused evolutionary change.

Mendel found that crossing a tall pea plant with a short one produced descendants of which ¾ were tall and ¼ short. There was no middle ground of some plants in between the tall and short as he had hoped. The dominate gene accounted for ¾ of the plants and the recessive gene for ¼. They were like one parent or the other in each characteristic but not like both at the same time.[1]

As a monk, Gregor Mendel would have studied the word of God, so he should have known what the scriptures say about such things. In Genesis we read: "And God said, Let the earth bring forth the living creature *after his kind*, cattle, and creeping thing, and beast of the earth *after his kind*: and it was so. And God made the beast of the earth *after his kind*, and cattle *after their kind*, and every thing that creepeth on the earth *after his kind*: and God saw that it was good (Genesis 1:24–25; emphasis added).

The Bible says that each kind of animal brings forth after its own kind. There is no room for changing from one kind to another. Mendel ended up supporting what the Bible says with his experiments, though he failed in his hope that crossbreeding would produce evolutionary change. Indeed the crossing of different animals usually results in sterility in the offspring. For example, horses and donkeys can have offspring, and these are called mules, but mules cannot reproduce, and therefore are not a new species.

Mendel did prove, however, that some traits could be repressed for a number of generations. When they did show up, these recessive traits would seemed new, but the genes were already there; they were simply hidden. Indeed, it has been found that we use only about a tenth of the genes we have at any one time. The rest are hidden or recessive or turned off, just waiting for the right circumstances to turn them on again.[2]

The prophet Moses knew that animals bring forth after their own kind, but it took Gregor Mendel to prove it using science before people would believe what Moses said. How much farther we would be in genetics if scientists had gone to the scriptures for basic scientific ideas instead of to natural philosophers? Anyway, the scientists are moving toward catching up with the prophets, at least in genetics. Good for them.

Notes

1. Frank Eisenhower and Alexander Schleiffer, "Biography of Gregor Mendel," IMP Bioinformatics Group, http://mendel.imp.ac.at/mendeljsp/biography/biography.jsp.
2. "Gregor Mendel," ThinkQuest, http://library.thinkquest.org/20465/mendl.html.

6

Aliens in Prophecy— We Are Not Alone

In the Middle Ages, at least in some countries, the earth was thought to be a sphere. This was not because the Bible said it was a sphere, but because the idea came from the ancient Greek philosophers. Aristotle said that the eclipses of the moon showed the shadow of the earth to be round. The philosophers also noticed that the North Star was higher in the sky the farther north you went. This meant they were traveling on a bent surface and that the earth was round. Also, ships going out to sea went below the horizon. Again the surface of the sea was bent. The Earth was round.

Now this would have been fine if they had left it at that. But then they went on to say the earth was the middle of the universe. (Some people now say the universe is infinite and therefore where you are is relative and anywhere you are can be called the center of the universe, but that is another discussion.) Stephen Hawking said of Aristotle's ideas on this subject: "Aristotle thought the earth was stationary and that the sun, the moon, the planets, and the stars moved in circular orbits about the earth. He believed this because he felt, for mystical reasons, that the earth was the center of the universe, and that circular motion was the most perfect."[1]

Where did he get his "mystical reasons"? It just sounds a little like thinking so highly of yourself that you put yourself in the center of the universe. Continuing from Hawking: "This idea was elaborated by Ptolemy in the second century A.D. into a complete cosmological model. The earth stood at the center, surrounded by eight spheres that carried the moon, the sun, the stars, and the . . . planets."[2]

Like glass balls with the sun and planets stuck in them, these spheres circled the earth. The outer sphere contained the stars, which all moved together. (If they all moved together there must be something connecting them, right? This was the invisible sphere.) Anything beyond the outer sphere was unknown but it made a good place for God to live.

In the Middle Ages, the Catholic f accepted Ptolemy's model of the universe, and it became church doctrine. But as Copernicus and Galileo came up with other ideas of what the universe was like, they were persecuted by the church for disbelieving its doctrines. In this case we are sure the church made a mistake. They chose to follow Ptolemy rather than prophets. Perhaps this was because there were no prophets around at the time. Perhaps they should have stayed with the scriptures.

What did the Prophet Joseph Smith have to say about this? He said that many worlds have been created by God and peopled with his children (see D&C 76:24). God not only created this world, but many others as well. As scientists have studied the universe, they have not discovered the spheres that Ptolemy talked about. Rockets have gone around the moon and some planets and have not run into any invisible sphere yet. Not only that, but recently they have discovered that there are planets around other stars. The Prophet Joseph said there were other worlds there and now scientists are finding them.

An organization has been set up called Search for Extra Terrestrial Intelligence (SETI). Millions of dollars have been spent on machines to listen for radio signals from outer space. Millions more have been spent on sending messages into space. Anyone can put a message together and have it broadcasted to the stars. At this writing it only costs ninety-nine dollars to send five pictures or a five minute video. Just contact talktoaliens.com or deepspacecom.net to make the arrangements. What a change from believing our solar system is the only creation of God.

Of course there may be another way to contact extraterrestrial beings. Most people use a technique called prayer. This goes with the assumption that the extraterrestrials are telepathic or else have very sensitive instruments. God says he knows all things, so one way or another he can hear us. Should not God be called an extraterrestrial? He does not live on planet Earth. That sounds like an extraterrestrial to me.

We have records of a number of people who have been visited by glowing beings from somewhere else. These beings are called angels. Angels are also extraterrestrials. Should we not make the most of our contact with them? Science fiction authors write about meeting advanced races that are far beyond us in wisdom and knowledge and how we can benefit from that contact. God and angels are advanced extraterrestrials and are trying to give us the advantage of their superior wisdom and intelligence, but we do not listen very well. The Prophet Joseph said we should listen to God and his angels and not be so afraid of these extraterrestrials.

Notes

1. Stephen Hawking, *A Brief History of Time* (New York: Bantam Books, 1998), 2.
2. Ibid.

7

Creation According to Prophets— Eternal Elements

God is a creator. The Bible tells us that he made the earth and all things on it (see Genesis 1). Many people have taken this to mean that God created everything that exists, from that which did not exist. That is, he created the very elements from nothing. They think that God's process of creating is to make something from nothing.

Modern science gives us a law or principle that matter can neither be created nor destroyed. It may only be changed and made into something new or different. If you burn wood, the matter is not destroyed it is merely changed into ashes and smoke. The matter is still there. You may think that a nuclear bomb destroys matter when it goes off, but this is really not so. A bomb may change matter to energy, making it take a different form, but this is not destroying the matter, for a cyclotron can change energy back into matter. Matter and energy, like water and steam, are the same thing, just in different forms. Einstein, in his famous equation $E=mc^2$, makes energy and matter equal. Science knows of no matter being created or destroyed. How then was the Creation accomplished?

I have a brother who is a sculptor. He takes a slab of wet clay and shapes it into, well, mostly horses and cowboys, though he can make other things as well. He makes works of art. We say that he *creates* a statue. You may notice that he did not create the clay, but we still say he created the statue. By working with the clay and changing its shape he changes a slab of wet clay into a beautiful statue. Could it be that when

God was creating the earth he did the same thing my brother does with clay? Could God have taken existing materials and organized them into the earth as we know it where mankind can live?

If God created the earth from nothing, then why didn't he bring it into being in a finished and perfect form, instead of having to do all that extra creating of plants, animals, and people, even after the creation of the elements? It would have been more efficient that way. God should be efficient, shouldn't he?

Also, if God is perfect, then his creation should have been perfect. Adam and Eve would have been perfect, and so they would not have eaten of the forbidden fruit after being told not to eat it. The earth now is certainly not perfect. A perfect God would not have made an imperfect earth, if he started from nothing. But, if God started from materials that were already in existence, then the materials themselves may have been flawed. Thus the imperfections were not from mistakes God made, but from flaws in the materials he used. God is not yet finished with his creation. He may yet perfect it and us.

The first sentence in the Bible says God created the earth (Genesis 1:1). This can be looked at two ways. Either God brought the earth into existence from nothing or this is a title sentence telling what God is going to do. As a title sentence, it would mean that God was going to tell next how he went about creating the earth. That is, he began by making a division of wet and dry, light and dark. Then he began preparing the earth to support plants, animals, and mankind.

Science fiction fans will have read about something called terraforming. Terraforming is to the process of changing an alien planet so that it will support human life. God terraformed a planet and made it into a usable earth; he did not make the earth from nothing. He started with a dark ball of mud covered by water and from that he created a place fit for men to live. Of course men have messed it up some since, but it is still a good place to live.

We have been commanded to become as much like God as we can be. Matthew said, "Be ye therefore perfect, even as your Father which is in heaven is perfect" (Matthew 5:48). If we are here to practice being like God, and God created the earth from nothing, then we should be having experiences in creating something from nothing. No one has ever had such an experience that I know of. If, on the other hand, God created the earth by organizing existing elements into a planet people can live on, then we have lots of practice in this kind of creation. We create houses, churches, roads, and we till the land. We change almost everything around us to be the way we want it. We create the things we use in the same way God created the earth, by taking raw materials and changing them to make them useful.

The Prophet Joseph Smith said, "The elements are eternal" (D&C 93:33). They have always existed and they will always exist. He wrote this back in the 1830s. Scientists have come to the same conclusion. Science is starting to catch up with him even if some religions have not. Joseph explained that if anything has a beginning, then it will have an end. If God created the earth from nothing, then it had a beginning and it (and we) will have an end. If we were created from nothing, we will eventually end up as nothing. I think that is sad. I don't want to be nothing.

8

The Growing Universe

In the Middle Ages, the universe shrunk to the size of the solar system, or at least people thought it did. People saw the sun and the planets moving against the background of stars and supposed the stars were all just a little beyond the planets.[1] As technology began to grow and telescopes were invented, the universe began to get bigger. About the year 1900, the entire known universe was our own Milky Way Galaxy.[2] As instruments got better, we discovered there were other galaxies outside the Milky Way. Eventually we came to the conclusion that if the big bang was about 14.4 billion years ago and since the speed of light is as fast as anything can go and remain in the universe, then we were sure the universe was about 29 billion light years across. The universe kept getting bigger and bigger.

Then we ran into a problem. The big bang could not have given us the universe as we see it.[3] When we look at quasars, we find they are all between 12.5 and 13.5 billion light years away. This means they are 12.5 to 13.5 billion years old. Of course, according to the big bang theory the universe would have been only about a couple of billion light years across that long ago. But when we look at quasars, they are in every direction we can see, instead of all in a ball just 2 billion or so light years across. In order for the big bang theory to work, they should all be in one spot in the sky smaller than the moon. There is a problem here. The universe is too big for the big bang to have made it all just 14.5 billion years ago. Must we say good-bye to the big bang theory?

Not to be deterred, scientists came up with what they call inflation, to try to save the big bang theory. They say that when the universe was "10^{-35} seconds old it underwent inflation, doubling in size 100 times [or 1000 times], effectively instantaneously."[4] Why this should be so or how it happened I have not been able to discover. But it does supposedly save the big bang theory. They get around the speed of light limit by saying that soon after the big bang, the laws of the universe that we know had not yet formed, so at that time matter could go faster than the speed of light. It is a bit of a stretch, but the theory seems to remain intact. If you stretch the universe back according to the original idea of the big bang, without this inflation, you get a universe at least 2.9 trillion light years across and well over 1.5 trillion years old. That was a long time ago. No wonder they invented inflation even though there was no reason for it. If the size of the universe determines how old it is, and the universe is discovered to be bigger than we originally thought, then it must be older than we thought as well. I see no reason for inflation here.

Since the Hubble satellite went into operation, the universe has increased in size 100 times (or 1000, since there are no rules to govern it). Will that be the end or will we eventually find that the universe is infinite? The Prophet Joseph Smith wrote that the creations of God are never ending (Moses 7: 30). He said, quoting the Lord, "Worlds without number have I created," (Moses 1:33) and in a song by William W. Phelps, a follower of Joseph Smith, we sing "There is no end to matter; There is no end to space."[5] In 1831, the universe was thought to be the size of the solar system, but Joseph Smith was saying that it is infinite. The scientists are trying to catch up with the prophets again.

Notes

1. Hawking, *A Brief History of Time*, 3.
2. Steven L. Goldman, *Science in the Twentieth Century: A Social-Intellectual Survey*, (Chantilly, VA: The Teaching Company, 2004), 2:29.
3. Ibid., 2:49.
4. Ibid., 2:60.
5. "If You Could Hie to Kolob," *Hymns,* 284.

9

The Origin of Things—Little Bangs and White Holes

Another thing scientists say is that the universe is still expanding. Scientists have been saying this for some time. Everything is moving farther and farther apart. Not only is it expanding, but the rate at which it is expanding is increasing.[1] Joseph Smith said, quoting the Lord, "there is no end to my works" (Moses 1:38). God continues creating within infinite space using the infinite amount of matter at his disposal. I realize that we cannot really understand what it means to be infinite, but when you speak of the creations of God and the size of the universe, then infinite is the only word that gives the true meaning of it. Joseph knew this, and perhaps the scientists are finally coming to that conclusion also. We can hope so.

For many years there was a disagreement between those who followed the big bang theory and those who followed the steady state theory. We have talked about the big bang and dismissed it, so now lets talk about the steady state theory. The steady state theory says that the universe is now as it has always been. It is infinite in both time and space. The finding of quasars showed that the universe is much older than the big bang theory says it should be, but, at the same time, it shows that it once had quasars, but that it no longer has them, that we can see. It may be infinite, but it changes over time. This caused the scientists to throw out the steady state theory. I have already thrown out the big bang theory so what is left to replace these two theories? If the universe is infinite in time, expanding, and increasing in its rate of expansion, then by now everything should have cooled down to a heatless death of the universe, but it hasn't. Is there an answer to this? I think there is. How about another theory?

The answer to this lies in looking at quasars in a different way. Quasars are ancient sources of great amounts of matter and energy. They spew their matter and energy out into the universe. As we look back into the past we find galaxies being formed during the same time we find quasars in existence. Today we find that galaxies are finished entities and that quasars are no longer working, except perhaps in a small way in the centers of galaxies. Could it be possible that quasars are the machines or mechanisms that build galaxies? When galaxies were coming into being, there were quasars. Now, no more galaxies are being formed and there are no more quasars. Is that coincidence or cause and effect?

How does this provide us with a new kind of steady state theory? We need to look at the universe as scientists have said it exists to see where this may fit in.

1. Galactic clusters are bound by gravity. The galaxies in a cluster are not getting farther apart. They are bound together by gravity.
2. It is the space between these clusters that is expanding. Galaxies and clusters maintain their integrity. The expansion of the universe is happening out in space between the clusters.
3. Space or vacuum is not completely empty. It contains potential. This potential is sometimes called dark energy, quintessence, or the Higgs Field.
4. Quantum theory tells us that particles are popping into and out of existence all the time in what we think is empty space. It is also thought that the spreading of this Higgs Field is what is pushing and spreading the galaxies farther apart.

Now, if quasars made a batch of new galaxies about 14.5 billion years ago, what did they make them out of? Where do quasars get the stuff they bring into the universe? Could it be from the energy or potential found in this Higgs Field? If you could put a hole in the Higgs Field, what would come out? Would it be the material and energy to make a galaxy?

Some of you may have recognized that this seems to contradict what I said previously about matter and energy never being created or destroyed. However, we do not know just what the Higgs Field is. Perhaps it is another substance that is just another form of matter and energy. At any rate, the quasars are no longer around, so we could still say that nothing has been created or destroyed lately.

Instead of just one big bang, there could have been a lot of little bangs called quasars. Each quasar could be the beginning of a galaxy, or group of galaxies. If so, then we cannot know how far in the future it will be before God starts poking more holes in the Higgs Field to start a new round of creation. If you do not believe in God, you could say we do not know how long it will be until the Higgs Field stretches enough that it tears apart and new quasars are formed. Would a new batch of quasars spew out the stuff to start making new galaxies? How much room do you need between galaxies before God can start making more galaxies for his children to inhabit? I do not know, but in this way the Lord's course could be an eternal round of creation, refinement, and creation again (see 1 Nephi 10:19). As the universe expands, he creates more matter and energy using quasars to bring new galaxies into the universe, and using the galaxies to create new places for his children to live. It makes sense to me.

Notes

1. Goldman, *Science in the Twentieth Century,* 3:90.

10

The Theory of Relativity—Just a Matter of Time

Einstein is a man many people would call a genius. About the year 1905, he came up with the theory of relativity. Among other things this theory told us that time is just another dimension in addition to the dimensions of space. There is width, breadth, height, and time. Time and space are so connected that the word space-time is now common. One aspect of time-space this means is that the faster you move in space, the slower you move in time. The slower you move in space, the faster you move in time.

For example, if we send someone to another star in a ship that goes at nearly the speed of light, we will find that on returning he will not have aged as much as the people who stayed here on Earth. By Earth time, he may have been gone four years but by the clocks on his ship he may have been gone only two years. This seems strange, but experiments have shown that it really does happen. The faster you move, the slower time goes for you. It is not logical, but it happens.

Now let us look again at the writings of the Prophet Joseph Smith. Did he have anything to say about relativity and the changing of time according to the speed you go? When asked the question, "Is not the reckoning of [time] according to the planet on which [beings] reside?" He replied, "I answer, Yes" (D&C 130:4–5). Each planet in our solar system, or any other solar system for that matter, would have a different measure of time according to how fast they were moving around their stars and by how fast the stars were moving around their galaxies. Therefore, each planet's time would be a little different than the others.

We also find from the Prophet Joseph Smith this statement: "I say unto you, [God] hath given a law unto all things, by which they move in their times and their seasons; And their courses are fixed, even the courses of the heavens and the earth, which comprehend the earth and all the planets. And they give light to each other in their *times* and in their seasons" (D&C 88:42–44; emphasis added). The planets each have their own time and Einstein tells us this comes because of the speed at which they move. The speed of their movements determines the speed of their time.

Perhaps you think the Prophet Joseph is just talking about time being measured by the rotation of the planets around the sun. Some have thought of it this way. To disabuse you of this notion, let us look in a work by Joseph Smith, first published in 1851 and then revised and republished in 1878—the Pearl of Great Price. In it we read the following: "The planet which is the lesser light [the moon] . . . is above or greater than that upon which thou standest in point of reckoning [the earth], for it moveth in order more slow" (Abraham 3:5). The moon orbits the earth so it goes the speed of the earth plus its own speed orbiting the earth. It moves faster than the earth, so how could it be said to move more slowly? Could it be that here the Prophet means its measurement of time is slower than time as measured on Earth? It moves faster, so its time is slower, just as the theory of relativity says it should be.

The Prophet Joseph quoted Abraham, saying, "Now the set time of the lesser light (the moon) is a longer time as to its reckoning than the reckoning of the time of the earth upon which thou standest" (Abraham 3:7). Thus we see that the time of the moon is slower than that of the earth. The reason for this is simple. As Einstein has shown, the faster a planet moves, the slower it's time is. The moon not only moves as fast as the earth but spins around the earth, so it moves faster than the earth, therefore its time must be slower.

From this we are left with the conclusion that Joseph Smith (or whoever he got his information from) knew about relativity before Einstein figured it out in 1905, for the Doctrine and Covenants and the Pearl of Great Price were both published in the 1800s. The prophets were again ahead of science, but the scientists are catching up. Einstein was a smart guy, and he figured it out.

The Prophet Joseph also gave us the Book of Abraham. We read from Facsimile #2 in the Book of Abraham, "Celestial time signifies one day to a cubit" (Figure 1). Abraham measures a day by a cubit. A cubit is a measure of distance and a day is a measure of time. Now when Joseph wrote this back in the 1840s, some people thought he was just making up something strange and hard to understand by comparing distance and time. Now Einstein has taught us better with his concept of space-time. Einstein put them together in 1905, while Joseph Smith (or his sources) knew about space-time long before Einstein came along. Isn't that interesting?

11

What Is the Matter with Spirits?

Science tells us that many things are organized in a spectrum or continuum. Things are not all black and white but come in many shades of gray. Temperature goes from cold to cool to warm to hot. Speed goes from slow to fast and all speeds in between. Many things run in a continuum.

One of the things that comes in a continuum is matter itself. We all know about the three states of matter that are taught in school: solid, liquid, and gas. When things are cold enough they are solid. If you add heat they become liquid. Add more heat, and they become gas. Logically, it would seem like adding something to what is already there would make the original thing more solid as empty spaces are filled. But the opposite appears true. Adding heat to matter makes it less substantial and more fluid, moving it from solid to liquid to gas. But this is not the end of the spectrum.

If more heat or energy is added, matter is changed into plasma. The atoms break down and the nuclear forces that hold them together no longer work. They become a step beyond a gas and a step closer to light. With enough energy, the atoms produce photons or light. Just as an iron rod begins to glow and give off light as it is heated, if enough heat is added, it changes its nature toward light itself. But the spectrum may not end there.

There may be a step beyond light that we will call spirit. Spirit matter is that substance of which spirits are made. It is beyond light. So the spectrum of matter goes from solid to liquid to gas to plasma to light to spirit, each one becoming thinner or more tenuous as more energy is added. Perhaps it would be more accurate to say that it becomes more energetic and better able to do things. It only seems thinner and more tenuous because our senses can no longer perceive all of it. It may actually be growing in substance. Einstein says that the closer to the speed of light you get, the more massive you become. You collect more energy and more mass the faster you go. When you reach the speed of light, you theoretically have infinite mass. I wonder where all that mass is.

Now we know that matter, light, and energy are all the same thing, just in different forms. Einstein said so with his famous $E=mc^2$. I will add spirit to the list also. Now the Prophet Joseph Smith wrote about this in 1843. He said, "There is no such thing as immaterial matter. All spirit is matter, but it is more fine or pure, and can only be discerned by purer eyes; We cannot see it; but when our bodies are purified we shall see that it is all matter" (D&C 131:7–8).

When I was younger, I heard in a history class that one of the questions medieval Christian scholars contended about was, "How many angels could dance on the head of a pin?" At the time I thought it was a silly question. Now I know that I just didn't understand the question. If I had understood it, I would have known that it was dealing not with angels so much as with the nature of spirit matter.

Light is about halfway between regular matter and spirit matter, so it has some of the characteristics of each. We can see it when it hits something and know it is there, but we cannot touch it, hold it in our hands, or see it moving. Light has no mass that we can detect. This means that we should be able to put any number of photons in the same place. If angels are made of spirit matter, then it should be possible to put an infinite number of angels in the same place for they would simply pass through each other.

What does this have to do with the teachings of the prophets? Joseph Smith taught that before the world was made, all the spirit children of God were present at a Grand Counsel in heaven. At this one meeting we all were taught the plan of salvation and given a choice of whether we would follow it or reject it. There have been about 68 billion people who have lived on the earth up until this time, and we have at least a thousand years more to go. Let's round the number of spirits off to about a hundred billion in all. That's a nice round number. There was also one-third of God's spirit children who chose not to come to Earth as we did. So let's make it a 150 billion in that big counsel meeting. How could they all possibly fit into one meeting place? How could they all hear and participate? There are two ways, neither of which was known to science in the days of Joseph Smith.

In the days of Joseph Smith there were no loud speakers or sound systems. At that time preachers had to have good lungs to make themselves heard to even a small congregation. There was no television or internet that would allow large numbers of people to hear a single speaker, yet Joseph said that a 150 billion people were in one meeting. He may not have known how it could happen, but we do. Electronics is one way to solve the problem, but there is another solution.

If you go into a darkened room, take a number of flashlights, and set up the flashlights so they are all shining through the same "empty" space in the room, you will find that one beam of light does not interfere with the others. Light moves through other light without affecting it. If many beams of light can be in the same place at the same time, then why couldn't many spirits be in the same place at the same time? It would not be a matter of crowding together because just as spirit goes through regular matter so it goes through other spirit matter also. That is the key. Now we have two ways that God could hold this miracle meeting of 150 billion spirits, neither of which was known about in the days of Joseph Smith. He must have known something others did not know at that time. Spirits are made of matter so pure and refined that we cannot see them with our natural eyes.

12

The Mortality of Mankind— Death Comes Unexpectedly

According to the Bible, Adam would have lived forever if he had not eaten of the forbidden fruit. With Eve's help he did eat the forbidden fruit, and so he did eventually die. But he did not die immediately. In fact the Bible tells us he lived for 930 years before he died. The Bible records that many others lived eight and nine hundred years before they died (see Genesis 5). It was not until after the flood in Noah's time that the life span of people began to shrink, each generation getting older and dying more quickly than the last one. Perhaps inbreeding caused the aging process—at least it can cause other problems. Now what has science to say about people living to be thousands of years old?

There are single-celled organisms that live in great numbers on the earth. These include amoebas and paramecium. They are found everywhere. One interesting thing about some of them is that they are immortal. They can be killed by violence, it is true, but unless they are killed, they live forever. These little critters multiply by dividing into two new cells. There is no way to tell which one was the original cell. There may even still be some of them around that were here when Adam was in the Garden of Eden! If these little cells are immortal then why are we not immortal also? Scientists say we evolved from such cells and immortality would certainly have a survival value, so why doesn't everything live forever? If a little microorganism can be immortal, then why not us?

Perhaps Adam eating that fruit had something to do with it. I wonder if, before Adam ate the forbidden fruit, he rubbed some cells off his skin and so those cells did not get a dose of the poison apple or whatever fruit it was. Those cells would then be immortal as some microorganisms are.

How else could such a valuable trait as immortality have been lost in the process of evolution?

Just as single-celled amoebas divide to make new cells, so do the cells in our bodies. If the cells in our bodies can divide and continue their existence, then our bodies should last forever, with new cells replacing old ones. We should be immortal. But we aren't.

Scientists usually say that ancient peoples lived much shorter lives than we do now. They base this on how long people living in primitive cultures live now. (Except, of course, in places like Peru and rural Japan where some people live a lot longer than we do.) Among many Christians, the Old Testament is taken as fictional stories that have no basis in fact. Joseph Smith took the Old Testament as real history.

13

The End of Time—For Real

One day, as I was listening to a lecture by Robert Hazen, I heard an interesting statement. He said that "entropy determines the direction of time."[1] Stephen Hawking puts forth the same idea when he speaks of time's arrow.[2] It means that there are processes that are not reversible because time moves in just one direction: forward. Entropy, or the degradation of matter, is the natural result of being in a universe where time is constant and moving forward. For example, burning a piece of paper seems natural and right, but to unburn a piece of paper just does not make sense. Entropy would have to be reversed, and we do not know how to do that. These kinds of processes are connected with time and only go one way.

Recall Einstein's theory about how speed and time are related. He was mostly right, but there is something that does go the speed of light all the time, and that is light itself. If light moves at the speed of light, then it should stop and not go anywhere, for its time is stopped. In truth, light continues to shine, move, and interact with the universe. Einstein meant that no gross physical matter can go the speed of light. There are other things that can and do travel that fast, and we can observe them doing it. Therefore, I would argue that if you could reach the speed of light, then you wouldn't stop, you would simply change into light. Matter, energy, and light are interchangeable after all. Only light can go that speed so if you went that speed, you would change into light or energy.

A further support for this is that light itself—that is the photons that make up light—can travel all the way across the universe. While everything around that photon would see it moving in time, the photon itself would experience no passage of time at all. According to Einstein's theory of relativity, a photon could move 15 billion light years and not experience any time passing, though 15 billion years would have passed for those watching it. This is what scientists have said, but what about the prophets? Have they mentioned anything about this interesting phenomenon?

In the year 1832, the Prophet Joseph Smith received a revelation from the Lord that the time would come when "Satan is bound and time is no longer" (D&C 84:100; see also D&C 88:110 and Revelation 10:6). How do you get rid of time? People talk often about the end of time, but they do not usually take it literally. Now the end of time is not the end of existence. Light exists, but it does not exist in time, for no time passes for it from its creation to its demise, yet we can see light and its effects all around us. Could the end of time for us be the Lord speeding up the elements of the earth and our bodies until we become like light? We would still be able to move and act and do things (as light does), yet for us, no time would pass at all. If you think about it, this could have advantages for us. No more aging, sickness, or death. Sounds almost like heaven, doesn't it?

I think it's interesting that when an angel comes to visit a person, he is usually described as being in a bright light. Christ and the Saints of olden times are drawn with halos around their heads—again, light is connected with them. When people almost die, but have come back from the dead, they speak of meeting a being of light who reviews their life and doings.[3] Have you not heard that "God is light" (1 John 1:5)? Does this mean that God has a body made of light? If so, then he is not in time as we are, but in eternity. That could be why, "All is as one day with God, and time only is measured unto men" (Alma 40:8).

The end of time may not be just figurative but literal, for we are told our bodies will be changed to become like Christ's glorious (light-filled?) resurrected body. Does this mean the elements of our bodies will become as energy or light and that we will be eternal beings and have no end? Does being glorified mean being changed into a being of light, literally? Entropy will have ceased for us, and we will be able to continue for ever and ever as God does. Time and entropy will stop for us, but love, learning, and work will not.

Notes

1. John E. J. Schmitz, *The Second Law of Life: Energy, Technology, and the Future Earth As We Know It*" (Norwich, NY: William Andrew, 2007), 47.
2. Hawking, *A Brief History of Time*, 145.

3. Raymond A. Moody, *Life After Life: The Investigation of a Phenomenon—Survival of Bodily Death* (New York: Bantam Books, 1976), 58.

14

A Theory That Evolves God—Think About It, but Don't Believe It

Science is big on the theory of evolution. I have studied it enough to know that evolution does not happen here on Earth. Mutations come at rate of a thousand bad ones for every good one. That means we are going downhill or de-evolving. Natural selection does not work because there are at least three different ways bad mutations can hide and spread in a population, and not be culled in the survival of the fittest.[1] What scientists call evolution is really just adaptation or the bringing out of hidden genes that are there already, not new or mutated genes. Only about 10 percent of the genes we have are in use at any one time. The rest are just waiting for conditions to be right for them to come out and be useful. But, anyway, in keeping with the theory of evolution, I will now tell you a theory of how God could have evolved in the universe. I do not believe it myself, but here perhaps it will help you believe in God.

First, Einstein has told us, and it has been proven experimentally, that the closer to the speed of light you go, the slower time flows. He said you could not reach the speed of light for time would stop.[2] You might think that if time stopped, movement would stop also. This is not so. Going the speed of light does not stop movement. Light itself goes the speed of light, but it does not stop. It continues to move through the universe. Time may stop for the photon of light, but the rest of the universe still sees it moving. Therefore the speed of light is attainable, for light goes the speed of light all the time.

Second, scientists agree that the direction of time is determined by entropy. Entropy is what makes evolution go downhill for us here on Earth. Things go from organized to chaotic. They get more and more messed up. Time's arrow goes only one way for us, and that is forward or perhaps I should say downward.[3]

Now suppose you could pass the speed of light. Scientists think that tachyons go faster than light, so it might be possible—if you were all-powerful and all-knowing, as God is—to travel faster than the speed of light. If you passed the speed of light, then entropy might be reversed. Instead of things becoming more chaotic, as they do here on Earth, things would naturally become more organized. It is only when moving faster than the speed of light that evolution would work. Of course we might have to change our bodies into light or some form of energy (or spirit) to go that fast. We know that matter can be changed into light or energy because scientists have done it. If we could move that fast, then our organization would increase. Evolution would happen.

When God comes to prophets, there is almost always a light or halo around him. The angels are most often described as being surrounded by light and wearing bright clothing. When people come out of near-death experiences, they often tell of going before a Being of Light where their life is reviewed. If the body of God is made of something like light or energy—which it would be if he were from a planet moving faster than the speed of light—then you would almost expect a brightness or light to be around him.

On a planet moving faster than the speed of light, evolution upward would be natural according to scientific law, and God could evolve into the greatest of beings. He could start as almost nothing, but because entropy is reversed when you go faster than light, he would become more and more organized, complicated, intelligent, and powerful. He would become the greatest being that could be. Surely he would eventually reach the place where he could reach into the slower-than-light places (like Earth), create a world, and put people on it. If you insist on a beginning for God, then here is one that fits your science. I do not believe it, but as a theory it makes more sense than the present big bang theory or steady state theories.

Notes

1. See William D. Stansfield, *The Science of Evolution*, (New York: Macmillan, 1977), 170, 176, 194.

2. See Joel Achenbach "The Power of Light," *National Geographic*, October 2001, 15.
3. Hawking, *A Brief History of Time*, 45.

Part II

Prophets Know the Future— Prophecies and Their Fulfillment

One of the amazing things about prophets is that they prophesy or foretell the future. How is it that the prophets can know what is to come in the future? They know because God tells them. How then does God know the future? I can think of two possible explanations. First, God is a master scientist, and second, God dwells in eternity.

Let us consider God as a master scientist. Most everyone has been in a high school science class and had to do experiments. Students are given chemicals, beakers, mixing bowls, and a set of instructions. Following the instructions they mix the chemicals and watch what happens. If the chemicals are pure and the instructions are followed exactly, the same thing will happen every time the experiment is done. The teacher already knows what reaction to expect and can grade the students based on whether they get the desired reaction. The laws of nature are exact enough that science teachers already know what will happen. They know that if you do certain things there will be certain results. In a way, they know the future.

In like manner, this earth may be thought of as a set of chemicals. All that happens on Earth is according to the chemicals used and the instructions given. What happens on Earth is a lot more complicated than what happens in a laboratory, but the earth also follows rules. Just as a science teacher knows what will happen in the students' experiment, so God knows what will happen on Earth. The science teacher designed the students' experiments and God designed the earth. Thus God knows the future of the earth.

The other possibility is that God dwells in eternity. We see the world in three dimensions: length, width, and thickness. We can look to the right or left of us, in front and behind us, and up and down. Another dimension is time or duration. We can only see things as they are right now. If our Christmas present will be under the tree tomorrow, we cannot look under the tree today and see our present there. We can only see a small slice of time at any one moment.

God, on the other hand, dwells in eternity. He is not bound by time as we are. God can look into the future and the past as easily as we can see to our right and left. When God looks at a person, he sees that person not only as he is now, but as he was in the past and as he will be in the future. He sees the person's full life, all at once. He knows the past, present, and future, and so he can tell us what will be. This is what the scriptures mean that say God knows the end from the beginning. When he begins a work, he already knows what the end of that work will be. Let us now look at some prophecies that the prophets have given us.

15

A Prophecy of Apostasy

A Falling Away

The Apostle Paul warned of an apostasy from the truth that would happen before the return of Christ in his glory. He said there would be a falling away before that great event (see 2 Thessalonians 2:3). People would fall away from the doctrine taught by Christ and the Apostles, and try to come up with their own ideas.

Luke, a missionary companion of Paul, told how this would begin and the two directions the apostasy would come from. He quoted Paul saying, "For I know this, that after my departing shall grievous wolves enter in among you, not sparing the flock. Also of your own selves shall men arise, speaking perverse things, to draw away disciples after them" (Acts 20:29–30). While the Apostles were living, they could detect the wolves that were trying to destroy the flock of God and could take steps to stop them. Once the Apostles had departed in death, the wolves would have free reign.

The wolves entering the flock may have been an allusion to the Greek philosophers that came into the church and because they were more educated, they soon took over the administration of the Church. They became the bishops and priests. After they had gotten into the Church, they began changing the doctrines. The Godhead became the Trinity. Repentance became penance. Anointing the sick for healing became anointing them unto death in extreme unction. The blessing of little children became the baptizing of little children. The Greek philosophers spoiled the Christian doctrine (see Colossians 2:8).

The second area of concern was that, among the followers of Christ, some would forget the gospel as given by Christ and the apostles, and start teaching their own perverse doctrine. This can be easily seen in the ancient inquisition. It can also be seen today in those groups that have started giving baptism and the sacrament to those who have not brought forth the fruits of repentance. In the "once saved, always saved" school of thought, you can sin all you want and still be saved in the highest heaven. Some organizations are even ordaining ministers through the mail rather than by the laying on of hands, as the scriptures direct. The righteousness or character of the minister is not even considered. If they have the money to pay the fee, they are considered an ordained minister. It will be plain to those who look that these churches have changed the ordinances and broken the everlasting covenant (Isaiah 24:1–6). The scriptures warned that this would happen, so we should not be too surprised.

False Christs and False Prophets

Jesus himself said that the time would come when there would be false Christs and false prophets who would deceive the people (Matthew 24:24). Indeed, the place of Christ was to be usurped by one who would sit in the temple of God as if he were God (2 Thessalonians 2:3–4). Jesus even foretold when this would happen. That is, when the apostles who were keeping the wicked in check through their preaching would be taken out of the way, the wicked would take over and that wicked one would be revealed, as he put himself into the position of God (2 Thessalonians 2:7–8). Without the true apostles of God, the false ones began to have free reign on the earth.

There have been many proclaiming themselves as Christ. None have appeared as the scriptures say, coming down from heaven in like manner as he went into heaven. There have been many saying they are prophets, but few have done the work of a prophet. You can recognize a prophet by what he does and the fruit he brings forth. The works and teachings of modern prophets will be studied more closely in the third section of this book.

Turning to Fables

The scriptures also give us some things to help us know how to recognize false Christs and those who would take us away from the true gospel of Jesus Christ. It is said that the people will not endure sound doctrine but after their own lusts shall heap to themselves teachers having "itching ears" (2 Timothy 4:3). If we look around now, we find there are many churches that are teaching things that are not sound doctrine. The people who hire these ministers are hiring them to teach what they want to hear. Some churches allow homosexuality among their members and even among their ministers. The Apostle Paul said those who practice homosexuality were worthy of death (Romans 1:24–32). How can those worthy of death for their sins be ministers? The Holy Ghost will not stay in an unclean tabernacle, so they cannot know the will of the Lord.

I even know of a person who "got saved" while living in adultery. I do not believe this can happen, but some churches teach that it can. These churches hire teachers who say what they want them to say, even if it contradicts scripture and common sense. This is evidence of apostasy.

Two Plain Signs of Apostasy

Paul also gives us two very plain things that were to show us that the Apostasy is real: forbidding to marry and commanding to abstain from meats (1 Timothy 4:3). Do you know of people who claim to be Christians that forbid people to marry? Do you know of church leaders that teach their congregations to be strict vegetarians? I would be very careful of such organizations, for these two things are given to us as clear signs of apostasy, according to the Apostle Paul. You can't get much plainer than that.

Denying the Power of God

Another thing that separates apostates from true disciples is having a form of godliness, but denying the power of God. We are told to turn away from such people (2 Timothy 3:5). They may go through the motions, but is the power of God shown in them? Do they have the Holy Ghost? Are the gifts of the Holy Ghost found in their lives? I do not mean the gift of echolalia. Some speak in tongues to God, but can they also speak to other people who do not speak English and have them understand? Can they understand other languages they have not learned? Can they prophesy and always have their prophecies come true? Have they seen or done miracles? Are the gifts of the spirit they claim to possess real or just pretend?

Jesus Christ was a priest after the order of Melchizedek. He ordained apostles and gave them the same power he had. Jesus said the apostles would do greater things than he had done. Do you have priests after the order of Melchizedek to lead you aright? Do you have apostles and prophets? The Church is to have a foundation of apostles and prophets (Ephesians 2:20). Without this foundation, it may fall. Apostles and prophets have the power of God. If they are not at the foundation, you may be denying the power of God. Christ was a priest after the order of Melchizedek. You need someone in this order of priesthood to keep you on the right track and keep you from denying the power of God. Denying priesthood power is a sign of apostasy.

The Saints Were Overcome

History tells us that early Christians went through hard times with persecution from the Romans and assaults from Greek philosophy, but did the Church endure these things and continue into our day? In Revelation we are told that the dragon and his beast were given the power to make war with the Saints and overcome them (Revelation 13:7). The war began when the apostles were still on the earth. Once they were removed, the Saints were overcome. Every kindred, tongue, and nation was put in the power of the dragon. The apostasy became complete, the Saints were overcome.

The Restoration

But this is not the end of the story. Luke speaks of the time when there would be times of refreshing and a restitution of all things spoken by the prophets (Acts 3:20–21). All that was lost with the death of the apostles would be brought back. It would begin with the coming of an angel who had the everlasting gospel to preach to every nation, kindred, tongue, and people (Revelation 14:6). In other words, all those who were overcome as spoken of in Revelation 13 would be taught the gospel again as shown in the next chapter (Revelation 14). There would again be true Apostles and prophets who had the priesthood power and taught the full gospel of Jesus Christ. I am glad of that.

16

A Prophecy of the Gathering of Israel

A Prophecy of Isaiah

In the book of Isaiah we are told, "In that day . . . the Lord shall set his hand again the second time to recover the remnant of his people" (Isaiah 11:11). The first time he recovered his people was when he brought them back from Babylon. The fulfillment of their first return to Jerusalem is recorded in the books of Ezra and Nehemiah in the Bible. We must look for a later time to find the second return of the Jews to Jerusalem. When Isaiah says "in that day," he usually means just before the Lord's second coming, or in other words, in our day. The Lord is to bring the Jews back to Jerusalem just before his second coming. This is another prophecy we have seen fulfilled in recent history.

Israel is now a country in western Asia, located on the eastern edge of the Mediterranean Sea. The modern state of Israel has its roots in a Jewish belief that the Jews would return to the land of Israel at some time in the future. This idea (called Eretz Yisrael) comes from Isaiah 11. This idea has been a concept in Judaism for over three thousand years. Just before World War I, many Jews had given up on the idea and wanted to remove the concept of a return to Jerusalem from their books. They did not see any possibility of it happening.

After World War I, the League of Nations approved what was called the British Mandate of Palestine with the intent of creating a "national home for the Jewish people." After Hitler tried to exterminate the Jews in World War II, the leaders of the nations wanted to give them a safe place to live. On May 14, 1948, the Jewish Provisional Government declared Israel's independence. By order of the United Nations, the Jews are now an independent nation in the land of Jerusalem, just as Isaiah said they would be thousands of years ago. The Jews are now gathering there from all over the world.[1]

The Lord said he would use the kings of the Gentiles to bring his people back to Jerusalem (Isaiah 49:22–23). It was the presidents and representatives of many countries in the League of Nations and later in the United Nations that began working for a national homeland for the Jews. In truth, it was the kings or leaders of the Gentiles that brought the Jews back to Israel.

Israel has remained an independent nation despite the efforts of some other nations to wage war on it and destroy it completely or drive the Jews into the sea. Israel's population continues to grow, and is now estimated at over 7 million. The prophecy of the return of the Jews to Jerusalem has been fulfilled in detail; just as Isaiah said three thousand years ago. Isaiah, as a prophet, knew things that others did not. He knew the future of Israel and the Jews.[2]

Notes

1. "Israel," Wikipedia, http://en.wikipedia.org/wiki/Israel
2. Ibid.

17

The Sealed Book

A Prophecy of Isaiah

The name "Ariel" is another name for Jerusalem. Because of this, some people think of the prophecy in Isaiah is about the Jews and Jerusalem, but a careful reading will show that it is about a place like unto Jerusalem (Isaiah 29:2). In verse 3, Isaiah speaks of preparing for war, and in verse 4, he speaks of this place like unto Jerusalem being brought down. It is to be conquered in war. Then what is to happen? The people that were brought down by war were to speak "out of the ground, and [their] speech shall be low out of the dust."

When was this to happen? Isaiah 29:10 gives us a clue. It would be when "the Lord hath poured out upon you the spirit of deep sleep, and hath closed your eyes: the prophets and your rulers, the seers hath he covered." After the destruction of this people by war, the people would close their eyes to the things of God. The prophets and seers would be covered, that they would not give the words of the Lord to men. It would be during a time of apostasy when the word of God would be scarce.

Then he gives a prophecy about a book: "And the vision of all is become unto you as the words of a book that is sealed, which are delivered [the word "men" is not in the original] to one that is learned, saying, Read this, I pray thee: and he saith, I cannot; for it is sealed: And the book is delivered to him that is not learned, saying, Read this I pray thee: and he saith, I am not learned" (Isaiah 29:11–12).

This book is to be part of the marvelous work and wonder the Lord will do among those whose lips honor the Lord, but whose hearts are far from him (Isaiah 29:13). In other words, the book will come in a time of spiritual darkness, when men claim to have the Lord, but do not. After the book comes forth, men will "increase their joy in the Lord, and . . . rejoice in the Holy One of Israel" (Isaiah 29:19).

When is all this to happen? Isaiah says, "Is it not yet a very little while, and Lebanon shall be turned into a fruitful field, and the fruitful field shall be esteemed as a forest?" (Isaiah 29:17). Lebanon has been irrigated and has already become a fruitful field. It must have happened before now.

Let us break things down and see what is to happen.

1. A place like unto Jerusalem is to be destroyed by war.
2. Those who were destroyed are to speak out of the ground.
3. They shall speak from a book that is sealed.
4. The words of the book (not the book itself) are delivered to the learned.
5. The learned cannot read a sealed book.
6. The book is delivered to him that is not learned.
7. The Lord will do a marvelous work and a wonder.
8. The deaf shall hear the words of the book.
9. Men will increase their joy in the Lord.

The Fulfillment of the Prophecy

1. The Book of Mormon speaks of a place called Zarahemla. It was the center of government for a small nation in America. This nation, whose citizens were called Nephites, was destroyed in a war by another nearby nation, the Lamanites.
2. When the Book of Mormon was found, it was buried in the ground. The words of the Nephites—their book—came out of the ground and from the dust.
3. When translating the Book of Mormon, Joseph said part of it was sealed, and he was forbidden to translate that part.
4. Martin Harris took a copy of some of the characters that were on the plates (not the plates themselves) and the translation Joseph Smith had made to New York. He said, "I . . . presented the characters which had been translated, with the translation thereof, to Professor Charles Anthon. . . . Professor Anthon stated that the translation was correct. . . . He said they were true characters. He gave me a certificate, certifying to the people of Palmyra that they were true characters, and the translation . . .

was also correct. . . . [He] asked me how the young man found out that there were gold plates in the place where he found them. I answered that an angel of God had revealed it unto him" (Joseph Smith—History 1:64).

5. "He then said to me, 'Let me see that certificate.' . . . He took it and tore it to pieces, saying that there was no such thing now as ministering of angels, and that if I would bring the plates to him he would translate them. I informed him that part of the plates were sealed, and I was forbidden to bring them. He replied, 'I cannot read a sealed book' " (Joseph Smith—History 1:65).
6. The book is given to Joseph Smith, an unlearned farm boy, and he is able to translate it through the gift and power of God. We have it with us today as The Book of Mormon.
7. By translating the Book of Mormon, Joseph was able to bring to pass a marvelous work and a wonder. The Book of Mormon is the keystone of the Church of Jesus Christ of Latter-day Saints.
8. Those who were spiritually deaf were able to read the words of the book and come to a knowledge of the truth.
9. The truth of the Book of Mormon has brought great joy to those who read it and understand the greatness and comprehensiveness of the Atonement of the Lord Jesus Christ. The joy of believers has increased in the Lord as they have learned more about him.

Thus we see that the prophecy of the sealed book has been fulfilled completely.

18

The Coming of Elijah

Elijah was one of the greatest prophets in the Old Testament. His ministry was during a period of apostasy in the kingdom of Israel. Ahab, the King of Israel, and his wife, Jezebel, were out to destroy the worship of Jehovah. Elijah almost single-handedly worked to stem the tide of wickedness. He performed miracles such as raising the dead and calling down fire from heaven. In the end, he was taken to heaven in a chariot of fire. He was such a great prophet that for generations after he was simply called "The Prophet."

The Prophecy

Malachi, the last prophet recorded in the Old Testament, spoke of a time when Elijah would return. He said: "Behold, I will send you Elijah the prophet before the coming of the great and dreadful day of the Lord: And he shall turn the heart of the fathers to the children, and the heart of the children to their fathers, lest I come and smite the earth with a curse" (Malachi 4:5–6).

The Prophet Elijah and the prophecy of his return are still remembered by the Jews. At the Passover feast, it is a custom among many Jews to reserve an empty seat for Elijah and to leave the door open for him to come in as they have their Passover feast. The Jews are looking for Elijah to come again before the Messiah comes (Bible Dictionary, "Elijah," 664).

The Fulfillment

On April 3, 1836, Joseph Smith and Oliver Cowdrey were in the

Kirtland Ohio Temple. On this occasion, they wrote the following: "Another great and glorious vision burst upon us; for Elijah the prophet, who was taken to heaven without tasting death, stood before us and said: Behold, the time has fully come, which was spoken of by the mouth of Malachi—testifying that he [Elijah] should be sent, before the great and dreadful day of the Lord come—To turn the hearts of the fathers to the children, and the children to the fathers, lest the whole earth be smitten with a curse" (D&C 110:13–15). Elijah has come again to prepare the earth for the second coming of the Lord Jesus Christ.

The work Elijah was to do was to turn the hearts of the fathers to the children and the hearts of the children to the fathers. This has been done. In the Church of Jesus Christ of Latter-day Saints, one of the responsibilities the members have is to search out the records of their deceased ancestors. In doing this, their hearts are turned to those whom they learn about. When the records are gathered, then baptism and the sealing of families together forever can take place. These ordinances are done by the living in the name of the dead.

The hearts of the fathers are turned to the children as the children perform the ordinances of salvation for their ancestors in the temple, thereby giving their ancestors a chance for eternal life with God. The hearts of the children are turned to the fathers as they learn about them and work to serve them. Since the days of Joseph Smith and Oliver Cowdrey, tracing one's genealogy has become one of the most popular hobbies in the world. Genealogical societies are sprouting up all over the world, and records are being collected. The work of Elijah is going forth. The prophecy has been fulfilled.

19

A Prophecy for Stephen A. Douglas

The Prophecy

The Prophet Joseph had many visitors in Nauvoo. One of those was Judge Stephen A. Douglas. Judge Douglas was a member of the Democratic Party and was rising in its ranks. He and Joseph became friends, but there was a caution to their friendship. The Prophet told Douglas on one occasion:

"Judge, you will aspire to the presidency of the United States; and if you ever turn your hand against me or the Latter-day Saints, you will feel the weight of the hand of the Almighty upon you; and you will live to see and know that I have testified the truth to you; for the conversation of this day will stick to you through life."[1]

The reason this was published then was because it looked like Mr. Douglas was going to run for president. The Saints wanted to remind him of what he could do for them and what would happen if he did not remain a friend to the Mormons. Mr. Douglas did not take the hint.

How Did Mr. Douglas React to the Prophecy by Joseph Smith?

In a speech he gave on June 12, 1857 he said:

> Nine tenths of [Mormons] are aliens by birth who have refused to . . . take the oath of allegiance or . . . [recognize] the government of the United States as the paramount authority in [Utah] . . . [Mormons] are bound by horrible oaths and terrible penalties, to . . . maintain the authority of Brigham Young, and the government of which he

> is the head . . . they will in due time . . . subvert the government of the United States, and resist its authority. . . . The knife must be applied to this pestiferous, disgusting cancer which is gnawing into the very vitals of the body politic. It must be cut out by the roots, and seared over by the red hot iron of stern, unflinching law.

Douglas asked to repeal the organic law of the territory of Utah on the grounds that they were alien enemies, outlaws, and unfit citizens of one of the free and independent states of the confederacy.[2]

The Mormons' Reply to Mr. Douglas

"By your own chosen course [you] have closed your chance for the presidential chair, through disobeying the counsel of Joseph." The prophecy was again printed to remind him of what Joseph had said and to give him a chance to repent. He did not repent.[3]

The Results

Right up until the election, it looked as if Mr. Douglas would overturn the prophecy of Joseph Smith and become president of the United States; however, as the votes came in, the results gave a different view of things. The results were as follows:

- Abraham Lincoln received 180 electoral votes winning 18 states
- Breckinridge received 72 electoral votes winning 11 states
- Bell received 39 electoral votes winning 3 states
- Stephen Douglas received 12 electoral votes winning 2 states—Missouri and New Jersey.[4]

When a prophet makes a prophecy, it is good to pay attention to it, for it will be fulfilled. If Mr. Douglas had had faith in Joseph, he could have avoided his embarrassing loss. As it was, he died about a year later, knowing that what Joseph had said was true. He had turned against the Saints, and the Lord had rewarded him accordingly. This prophecy of Joseph Smith has been fulfilled.

Notes

1. B. H. Roberts, *Comprehensive History of the Church of Jesus Christ*

of Latter-day Saints (Salt Lake City: Deseret News Press, 1909), 5:394.

2. Ibid., 5:396.
3. Ibid, 5:398.
4. Ibid, 5:396.

.

20

Prophecies of War

In Old Testament times, the prophets of Israel would often prophesy of the nations around Israel as well as about Israel itself. When a nation had done evil to Israel, the Lord would tell of their coming destruction in war. The Lord says "Vengeance is mine, and I will repay" (Mormon 3:15). We need not worry about wreaking vengeance on those who persecute us; the Lord will take care of that for us. The following are some examples of the prophecies made by Joseph Smith about the wars that Joseph said would come on the nation and people who persecuted and drove the Saints from the United States.

The Uncivil Civil War

In the year 1832, the Prophet Joseph Smith gave a prophecy on an upcoming war (see D&C 87:1–3). He said the war would begin with the rebellion of South Carolina, that the Southern states would be against the Northern states, and that this war would lead to the death and misery of many souls. He said that the Southern states would call on Great Britain for help. He also said that after this war, there would be many wars poured out on all nations, in other words—world wars. This prophecy was given about thirty years before the Civil War began. Students of history will realize that this prophecy has been fulfilled.

At the time this prophecy was given, it seemed a war was soon coming. But it did not happen since the politicians were able to make compromises to prevent it. The thought of war died down, but the prophecy remained. Then in 1843, the Prophet Joseph spoke of it again. This second prophecy made it clear that war was still coming. He said, "It may probably arise through the slave question" (D&C 130:12–13). I find it interesting that the war did not actually arise through "the slave question," but through the question of states' rights. Before the war was over, however, the slave question came to the forefront with the signing of the Emancipation Proclamation by President Lincoln. I guess that is why the Prophet said "may probably arise through the slave question," instead of it "will arise through the slave question."

Joseph said it would begin with the rebellion of South Carolina. South Carolina was the first state to declare secession from the Union. On April 12, 1861, the first shots of the war were fired at Fort Sumter in South Carolina. The Southern states were divided against the Northern states, and brother fought against brother and fathers against sons, so that death and misery did come to many souls. The South did call on Great Britain for help, showing them the war would cost them Southern cotton if the South lost. The prophecy was fulfilled, even if at a later date than at first believed. When a prophet speaks, it is good to listen.[1]

A Prophecy of Justice

In connection with the Civil War, Joseph once said to his enemies—who were driving his followers from Illinois and trying to kill him—that he could see their hearts and that they thirsted for his blood. Then he said: "I prophesy in the name of the Lord that you shall witness scenes of blood and sorrow to your entire satisfaction. . . . Many of you who are now present shall have an opportunity to face the cannon's mouth . . . and those people that desire this great evil upon me and my brethren shall be filled with sorrow because of the scenes of desolation and distress that await them."[2]

When the war with Mexico began, many of those very people went into the military. In 1846, Illinois was asked to supply men for the Mexican war. Many of the men Joseph was talking to went into the first and second regiments of the Illinois Militia under General Taylor. General Taylor's army of less than five thousand went against General Santa Anna and his twenty thousand men. Rushing into battle, the Illinois men soon found themselves in a gorge with Santa Anna's men holding the high ground on both sides. They were decimated. Later, in the Civil War, about twenty nine thousand men from Illinois died in the war, though only about six thousand died in action.[3]

A Prophecy against Missouri

On one occasion, Joseph Smith was in jail awaiting trial and had General Doniphan for his lawyer. While they were discussing Joseph's defense, a man came in, wanting to settle a debt with General Doniphan. To pay his debt, he wanted to give General Doniphan some land in Jackson County, Missouri. General Doniphan told him that when his partner returned, he would discuss it with him and let him know their decision. When the man left, Joseph said: "Doniphan, I advise you not to take Jackson county land in payment of the debt. God's wrath hangs over Jackson county. God's people have been ruthlessly driven from it, and you will live to see the day when it will be visited by fire and sword. The Lord of Hosts will sweep it with the besom [broom] of destruction. The fields and farms and houses will be destroyed, and only the chimneys will be left to mark the desolation."[4]

During the Civil War, parts of Missouri became supply stations and hideouts for the Confederacy. The Union put into effect "order number 11," requiring every person to leave the area, or the army would remove them. Mr. A. Saxey reported what he saw of Missouri in 1864 during the war: "I went down the Blue river, we found houses, barns, and outbuildings, nearly all burned down, and nothing left standing but the chimneys. . . . The country looked a veritable desolation."[5] Fire and sword had devoured the area—as the Prophet said—and only the chimneys were left standing to show what had been there. The Prophecy was fulfilled to the letter.

Notes

1. "Battle of Fort Sumter," Wikipedia, http://en.wikipedia.org/wiki/Battle_of_Fort_Sumter
2. Roberts, *Comprehensive History of the Church,* 2:256.
3. Roberts, *Comprehensive History of the Church,* 2:270–73.
4. Roberts, *Comprehensive History of the Church,* 1:538.
5. Ibid.

21

A Prophecy about Moving West

The Prophecy

"I [Joseph Smith] prophesied that the saints would continue to suffer much affliction and would be driven to the Rocky Mountains, many would apostatize, others would be put to death by our persecutors, or lose their lives in consequence of exposure and disease; and some of you will live to go and assist in making settlements and build cities and see the Saints become a mighty people in the midst of the Rocky Mountains."[1]

Anyone who knows the history of the Latter-day Saints will know that they left for the Rocky Mountains in 1847 and continued to gather there for many years. Some of the Saints did apostatize as a result of being driven from Nauvoo into the wilderness. They could not stand the persecution. Others died along the way from exposure and disease. Still others went on to Utah and began making settlements in Utah, Idaho, Arizona, and other western states. There the Saints began building cities and eventually grew to a numerous people in the midst of the Rocky Mountains.

I think it's interesting that the Saints went west not because they wanted to or in order to fulfill this prophecy, but because they were forced to leave the United States under threat of violence. This prophecy was fulfilled—for the most part—by the persecutors of the Saints and not by the Saints themselves. The Saints would have been happy to have stayed in Nauvoo had they been allowed to; however, they found they had to fulfill this prophecy whether they wanted to or not.

Notes

1. Roberts, *Comprehensive History of the Church,* 2:181.

22

The Martyrdom of Joseph and Hyrum Smith

In the year 1844, the city of Nauvoo, Illinois had grown to a large size—so large, in fact, that other cities were concerned about the political power of this city of the Saints. The Saints were also not trusted because of their clannish ways and unique religion. This brought persecution on the city. When the Nauvoo City Council destroyed a newspaper that was deemed a public nuisance, the Prophet Joseph, as mayor, was told to come to court for breaking Constitutional rights by forbidding the freedom of the press. The people never protested when Mormon presses were destroyed by those breaking the law, but when the city council followed the city law and destroyed a newspaper, then they complained. It was an excuse to capture Joseph Smith. Joseph knew if he put himself into the hands of his enemies, he would be killed. He decided on a plan of action. He said:

"The way is open. It is clear to my mind what to do. All they want is Hyrum and myself; then tell everybody to go about their business, and not collect in groups, but scatter about. There is no danger; they will come here and search for us. Let them search; they will not harm you in person or in property, and not even a hair of your head. We will cross the river tonight, and go away to the west."[1]

As he was leaving, a number of his friends and family came to him to try to get him to stay. They were sure they could trust Governor Ford, who had given his word he would keep the Prophet safe. Joseph then said, "If my life is of no value to my friends, it is of none to myself."[2] He turned around and came back to face trial at the hands of his enemies. He knew he would be killed, but he went back anyway. He said:

"I am going like a lamb to the slaughter; But I am as calm as a summer's morning; I have a conscience void of offense towards God, and towards all men. I shall die innocent, and it shall yet be said of me—he was murdered in cold blood.[3]

While Joseph was in Carthage Jail awaiting trial, a mob of about two hundred men with their faces painted black stormed the jail and shot and killed Joseph and Hyrum. Joseph's life had been in danger many times before, but he had never given up hope. This time he knew what was coming. It has indeed been said of him that he was murdered in cold blood. He was innocent of any crime, but suffered death at the hands of his enemies, sealing his testimony with his blood, as many other prophets and apostles had done before him (see D&C 135). His prophecy of his own death was fulfilled.

Notes

1. Roberts, *Comprehensive History of the Church,* 2:246.
2. Roberts, *Comprehensive History of the Church,* 2:247.
3. Roberts, *Comprehensive History of the Church*, 2:249.

Part III

New Doctrines from Modern Prophets

Many of the words of ancient prophets have been collected into the Bible. Since the Bible was created, men have been trying to interpret the Bible and understand just what it means, but they have not been very successful. Very few churches agree with each other. It seems it takes a modern prophet to understand and explain the words of the ancient prophets in the Bible. We need prophets to explain the scriptures to us.

With the coming of Joseph Smith, a new line of prophets has come into being. Part three of this book will discuss the new information that has come to us from this new line of prophets. It is the job of prophets to write scripture and tell us new things. These things should agree with the old things we already have, but they should go beyond what is already given. They should make sense and fill in gaps in the people's knowledge of the gospel. Let us now look at some of the things that we have learned from Joseph Smith and the line of prophets that followed.

23

Extending the Knowledge of the Creation

Was creation from nothing or from existing materials?

If I understand the general Christian belief, now held by the majority of Christians, they think that God created the world out of nothing. He spoke the word, and the earth came into being. Before that, it did not exist in any shape, form, or fashion. Genesis 1:1 says, "In the beginning God created the heaven and the earth." People take this to mean that God made the heaven (the sky) and the earth (the ground) out of nothing. Then we find that after the earth was created, God caused light to shine on it. He divided the water from the land. He then prepared the earth to bring forth plants and animals, and eventually man was on the earth.

After God supposedly called the earth forth out of nothing, it still took a lot of work to get it ready for his purposes. I wonder why God didn't just call the earth forth in a finished state. If he had, then all those extra things would not have needed a separate creation. That was not very efficient of him—he being perfect and all. But there may be another answer. Perhaps that first statement in Genesis was only an overview sentence for the story that was to follow. The first sentence said he created the heaven and the earth, and the next sentences showed how he brought about that creation. Perhaps the earth was already there, and the Creation story is simply telling what he did to make it fit for man to live there.

The scientific world today tells us that nothing is ever created out of nothing.[1] It may be changed from one form to another, but everything that now exists, came from what was already here. All the things that now exist have always existed in one form or another. Even proponents of the big bang theory say all the materials in the universe were there at the time of the big bang, they just do not know by what laws those materials were governed.

The Prophet Joseph Smith has told us that "The elements are eternal" (D&C 93:33). When God created the world, he simply organized the materials that were already there. When it says in Genesis that God created the world, we are not being told what he had already done, we are being told what God is going to do. The next few chapters then tell us of the Creation. The elements were already there, God just organized them by causing the land to divide from the water, preparing the earth to bring forth plants, which can then support the animals. Certainly Adam was made from the dust of the earth and not from nothing.

This doctrines of Mormonism agree with the scientists rather than the general Christian idea of Creationism. Christians in general think that this is part of the reason God is so great. God is so far above us that he can create things out of nothing and men are so low that we can't figure out any way he was able to do that. Is there anything that might give us a hint of which is right, modern Christian thought or science and Mormonism? Here is one idea.

How Do We Create Things?

I have an older brother who has taken an old barn and made it into a workshop. He now makes wooden bowls, dough rollers, ball bats, lamps, furniture, and many other things. When he starts to make something, the first thing he does is to search out the wood he is going to make it from. He has created many things, but he has not made them from nothing. He has made them from wood. Yet still, we say he created them.

Could it be that God makes things the same way? The materials for the earth were already there, and the genius of God was in knowing how to put them together in the right way to make what he wanted to make. We are here to learn to be like Christ and God (see 3 Nephi 12:48). If that is the way we make things here on Earth, then perhaps we are learning how God makes things. If God wants us to be like him, and he makes things from nothing, then we should be getting practice in making things from nothing. That is not happening, so I say that God created the earth from materials that already existed but were in a chaotic state. He organized it from a big ball of mud into a place where his children could live, just as we build houses to live in.

A Perfect Creation

Suppose that when God created the earth he started with elements or materials that were already there. Those materials would have certain characteristics within them. God did not create a perfect earth because the elements he used were not perfect. Isn't God still working with the earth to perfect it (and us)? Perhaps the road to perfection for the earth is to go through an initial organizing, as found in Genesis, then a change during the Millennium when Christ comes again and all creation will live in peace and harmony, the lion lying down with the lamb, and then a final change when the elements melt with fervent heat so that there is a new heaven and a new earth, made from the remains of the old one (Revelation 21:1). This would mean God is not yet finished with the Creation. If he began with unorganized materials, then we have a reason for the imperfections. God is still working to perfect the always existing materials of which the earth is made. It will not be finished until he changes this old earth and sky into the new heaven and the new earth that will exist at the end of the Millennium.

Joseph Smith has extended our knowledge of the Creation in that we now know it was not a creation from nothing, but that the materials had always existed and were organized by God.

The Creation of Man

When do we become ourselves? The usual thinking is that everything we are is created at the time of our birth—our bodies being created by our mothers, and our spirits appearing in our bodies about the time we are born. Before this, there was nothing. We know that the materials for the creation of a baby come from the things that a mother eats. The baby's body is not made from nothing, but from what already exists. It is just organized a different way. What about the spirit? Does God create the spirit at the time we are born? If so, then God creates something from nothing.

The Prophet Joseph Smith said, "Man was also in the beginning with God" (D&C 93:29). That is, all mankind existed as spirits before the world was created. This goes along with the Bible's assertion that God created all things as spirits before they were put on the earth (see Genesis 2:5). That is, there was a creation of spirits before there was a physical creation. How does it benefit us to know that there was a spiritual creation and existence before there was a physical one?

In my opinion, the idea that we come into existence at birth challenges the justice of God. Some people are born into homes where they hear the good news of Christ from the time they are born, where they have plenty of clothing, good shelter, all the food they want, and many luxuries. Others are born where they do not have a decent home, where they never hear of Christ, and where they are almost always cold, hungry, and in need. How could a just God start two people out in such different circumstances and yet require the same loyalty and obedience to him from both of them? To be fair, shouldn't they start out equal?

If God is to be just, and birth is when the complete creation of a person happens, then each of us should start out equally. If you were to run a race and the other person was put halfway to the finish line when it began, I think you would complain. How much worse would it be if you weren't even told there was a race until it was over, and all that you learned then was that you had lost? If a person didn't hear of Christ in this life, he wouldn't even know there was a race for salvation. It wouldn't be fair if he were only told on Judgment Day that he had lost the race.

On the other hand, if we lived as spirits before we came to Earth, then perhaps we had a choice and agreed to the place that we began the race. If we agreed to start the race with another person halfway to the finish line, then we could not complain that the other person got a head start. Perhaps we thought we could finish the race anyway. Thus we see that the justice of God required that we have an existence as spirits before we came to Earth. We lived before physical birth in the spiritual realm with God where we agreed to the conditions of Earth life. Our spirits were created long before our mortal birth. This means we agreed (or covenanted) with God to let him start us out where he wanted us to be. We had faith that he knew what would be best for us. We wanted the blessings that come from physical life, and to get them we agreed to come to Earth in whatever condition the Lord directed.

Logic concerning the justice of God tells us we lived before birth, but is there anything in the scriptures that agrees with this? We read that Christ existed with our Father in Heaven before the earth was made

(John 17:5). He was a spirit before the beginning of the earth. What about us regular people?

Jeremiah was ordained to be a prophet before he was born (see Jeremiah 1:4–5). The early members of the Church were also chosen to have the full gospel *before the foundation of the world* that they might gain salvation (see Ephesians 1:4; emphasis added). Also, the scriptures tell us that our spirits will return to God (see Ecclesiastes 12:7). They cannot return to a place they have not been to before. Thus we see that not only was Christ in existence before the world, but all of us regular people were as well. How else could we be called the children of God if not as his spirit children? We become children of our parents here on Earth when we are born. We became children of God when we were born as spirits in heaven. Otherwise we are not children but just creations or made things.

When I was younger, my older brother would make things for me. He became an artist making sculptures, so he had the skill to make slingshots, cane popguns, tree bark whistles, and such. These were creations of his. Right now, however, I do not know where any of those things are, and I doubt that he does either. Creations are not as dear to our hearts as children are. I would rather be a child of God than just his creation. The scriptures say we are his children, and I believe it.

I don't think that anyone will argue that angels existed before the earth was created. What some people seem to forget is that angels are just men with a message. The fact that angels are men is shown in Luke where two men in shining garments are later called angels (see Luke 24:4, 23). Angels are simply men who act as messengers from God to deliver his words to us. They are the spirits that were in heaven before the world and are of the same race as men, being also children of God. Thus we see that men were spirit children of God before the world was created. The Prophet Joseph Smith has added to our knowledge of creation, in telling us that we existed as spirits before we came to Earth.

The Fall of Man

Many people have read the Bible and have come to the conclusion that Adam and Eve are the cause of all our problems. There they were in the Garden of Eden, where everything was prepared for them. They did not need to work; food was ripe on the trees for the taking. There was little toil, no danger, and no trials. Everything was good and comfortable.

Then they blew it and ate that fruit God had forbidden them to eat, and in so doing brought on all of us the punishment of danger, toil, sickness, and death. Shame on them! Why didn't they leave things alone so we would all be happy living with them in Eden?

Joseph Smith said the Fall was part of the plan God had for this earth. God planned for the Fall to happen. In translating the Book of Mormon, the Prophet Joseph Smith revealed, "Adam fell that men might be" (2 Nephi 2:25). Without the Fall, the plan of God would be incomplete. This is opposite to what many people think the Bible says. Perhaps if we think about it and look in the scriptures a little more, we can come up with more evidence that good came from the Fall.

Now the first question we need to ask is, "Was the Fall a surprise to God?" We have it on good authority that God knows all things. He knows the end from the beginning, so when he began the creation of the earth he knew what the end of the creation would be. Did God, who is perfect, make a mistake? I do not think so. He knew if he put that tree in the garden and let the devil in, Adam and Eve would eat of it. So why did he do it? He could at least have put that tree over in the corner of the garden instead of the middle (midst) of it (see Genesis 2:9). He could have even forbidden Satan from going into the garden to tempt Adam and Eve. Heavenly Father didn't help them when he could have. Why not?

You will also notice that in the garden was the tree of life. All God would have needed to do to reverse the effects of the tree of knowledge, was to let them eat of the tree of life. He never allowed that. Instead of letting that happen, he put Cherubim and a flaming sword to keep them away from it (Genesis 3:24). It is beginning to look to me like God was stacking the deck against Adam and Eve. If that were so, why should we be angry with them for doing what they did when he put them in such a position that they could hardly do otherwise?

Now, why would God want the Fall to happen? The first (and most obvious) reason is that the tree was not just the tree of knowledge of evil. It was the tree of the knowledge of *good* also. By eating of that tree, Adam brought evil into the world, but at the same time he brought *good* into the world. In the Garden of Eden, things were not all good, as some suppose—they were neutral. God wanted good in the world; therefore, he allowed the Fall to happen. Evil just happened to come along with the good. We learn good from evil.

We do not put moral judgments on animals for what they do. When they kill other animals to eat, we just say that is their nature. They work by instinct, not by knowledge of right and wrong, good and evil. In the garden, Adam and Eve did not know right or wrong, good or evil. They were much like the animals in the garden. God wanted them, his children, to be more than mere animals. He wanted them to know good, even if a knowledge of evil had to come with it.

The next question is, "Can Adam and Eve be condemned for making a wrong choice, when they did not know good from evil?" How can they be held accountable when they did not know good from evil? Do we hold little babies accountable if they happen to push a book onto someone's head and send them to the hospital? No! We say they are not accountable, and neither were Adam and Eve, for they did not yet know good from evil. Eve was enticed by Satan. Just as people can entice animals into cages with food, Eve was enticed to eat the forbidden fruit. Can an animal be held accountable for a moral choice? Eve thought what she did would please God and make her more like God. I think she should have just as much right to the repentance process, after she learned good from evil, as the rest of us do, perhaps even more because she was deceived directly by Satan. Eve has as much right to repentance as we do.

What about Adam? Adam was not deceived (see 1 Timothy 2:14). He knew God had told him not to eat of the fruit. He also knew Eve had eaten it, and that she would be put out of the garden. Adam now had a choice to make—either stay in the garden without Eve or eat the fruit and go with her. God had also commanded them to multiply and fill the earth with their descendants. Adam could not multiply and fill the earth without Eve. He needed to break one commandment or the other. He decided to go with Eve. We ought to be glad he did, for we would not have been born otherwise. Adam took part in the Fall to forward the plan of God in the only way left to him, that is, by going with Eve that they might have children.

The Fall was not a mistake. God planned it so that we could learn good as well as evil and become more like him. And in truth, we can only learn good *from* evil. That is, it takes evil to make us know and appreciate the good. If we have nothing to compare good with, then how do we know it is good? It is like trying to tell someone what salt tastes like without saying salty. It just does not work. So we learn from Joseph Smith that God did not make a mistake in letting Adam and Eve fall, but it was all part of his plan for his children.

If Adam and Eve had not fallen, there would have been no need for a savior. We learn from the Apostle Peter that Christ was chosen as the Lamb of God to work out the Atonement before the foundation of the world (1 Peter 1:19–20). If Christ was chosen as the savior before the foundation of the world, then God knew the Fall was going to happen and a savior would be needed. It was all part of God's plan for the benefit of his children.

Christ brought about the Atonement. The purpose of the Atonement is to undo all the bad that happened because of the Fall of Adam and Eve. Therefore, when the Atonement takes effect, it will be as if the Fall never happened. All have sinned and come short of the glory of God and all can repent and regain the glory of God, Adam and Eve included. So do not judge them too harshly. God planned it that way.

Notes

1. Robert M. Hazen, *The Great Principles of Science*, (Springfield, VA: The Teaching Company) lecture 8.

24

Extending the Knowledge of God

The Bible tells us about God. Unfortunately people do not agree on what the Bible says about him. To make it easier, some churches make creeds that describe the God they worship. Most churches look on God as an incomprehensible, unknowable, wholly "other" trinity. In other words, these churches confess that they do not know God and do not understand him. This puts them in a difficult situation since it is "life eternal [to] know . . . the only true God, and Jesus Christ, whom [he] sent" (John 17:3). If God is unknowable, as some church creeds insist, then life eternal is beyond our reach, and we are all damned. If we do not have life, then we must have death. I think we want something better than that. We need to know God. Also, if God is not known or comprehended by these churches, why do they try to tell us all about him? This is plainly a contradiction.

One other thing they seem to think is that if they do not know or understand God, neither can anyone else. The Bible does not teach this. Enoch walked and talked with God as one man does with another. Abraham knew God so well he was called the friend of God. All the prophets have known God and have gained eternal life because they knew him. Prophets and apostles can extend our knowledge of God, for they know him. Ministers can't tell us anything about God if they think he is unknowable and beyond comprehension. I do not doubt he is beyond their comprehension for they are not prophets. We must look to prophets like Joseph Smith for help.

It has been said that God is a complete and absolute "other." My question is, why would the complete and absolute "other" be interested in us? Wouldn't he (or it) have better things to do than watch out for a bunch of bumbling incompetents like us, who won't listen to him and do what he says, even when it is clearly best for us? How could he love us if he is completely "other," without human emotion? Love is a human emotion. And how could he call us his children if he is completely other than we are? I cannot accept that God is that different from us.

We are commanded to be perfect as God is perfect (see Matthew 5:48). If that is the case, and if God is unknowable and a complete other, does that mean we are to become unknowable also and completely other than we are now? What purpose does life on Earth have if in heaven we will be completely different than we are now? We say some people are strange or eccentric. Does that make them unknowable? I do not want to be completely unknown and different. I think I would be lonely. Somehow that does not sit well with me.

Is the Godhead Three United Individuals or a Trinity?

Many Christians follow the ideas found in the Athanasian Creed about the nature of God. Athanasius lived from AD 296 to 373. Here is the portion of the creed on which many Christians base their idea of God:

> And the Catholic Faith is this, that we worship one God in Trinity and Trinity in Unity. Neither confounding the Persons, nor dividing the Substance. For there is one Person of the Father, another of the Son, and another of the Holy Ghost. But the Godhead of the Father, of the Son, and of the Holy Ghost is all One. . . . Such as the Father is, such is the Son, and such is the Holy Ghost. The Father Uncreate, the Son Uncreate, The Holy Ghost Uncreate. The Father Incomprehensible, the Son Incomprehensible, and the Holy Ghost Incomprehensible. The Father Eternal, the Son Eternal, and the Holy Ghost Eternal and yet they are not Three Eternals but One Eternal. As also there are not Three Uncreated, nor Three Incomprehensibles, but One Uncreated, and One Incomprehensible. . . . So the Father is God, the Son is God, and The Holy Ghost is God. And yet they are not Three Gods, but One God. . . . The Father is made of none, neither created, nor begotten. The Son is of the Father alone; not made, nor created, but begotten. The Holy Ghost is of the Father, and of the Son: neither made, nor created, nor begotten, but proceeding. . . . He therefore that will be saved, must thus think of the Trinity.[1]

And there you have it. I do not believe God is incomprehensible, but to me this creed certainly is. It does not make sense to me. In math, three does not equal one and one does not equal three. Nowhere in the Bible does it speak of a trinity, yet many Christians have accepted the doctrine of the trinity as truth.

I was once talking to a woman about religion, and she brought her minister to talk to me. I think she expected him to straighten me out. As we were talking about the nature of God, he started reading the above creed to me. He was reading it from a book by James E. Talmadge, a Mormon author, and he thought it was Mormon doctrine. He wanted me to see how confusing and silly it was. When I told him that the book was quoting the Athanasian Creed, where Christians (including him) get their ideas of the trinity, and that we disagreed with it, as he would have known had he read the whole page in the book, he was taken aback. After that, the woman who had brought him would no longer listen to him, and we had a good, profitable discussion. She learned some things. Perhaps her minister did too.

Christian ideas of the trinity are confusing; even Christians find themselves confused when they read where the idea of the trinity came from. So, can the Prophet Joseph Smith help us with this? Did he extend our knowledge of God and what he is really like? The Prophet said, "This is eternal lives—to know the only wise and true God" (D&C 132:24). To gain eternal life we must know God. What does Joseph say God is like? He did not just read and think about what God is like, Joseph had actual experience with him. If anyone should know, he should.

The Prophet Joseph Smith said of his first encounter with deity, "When the light rested upon me I saw two Personages, whose brightness and glory defy all description, standing above me in the air. One of them spake unto me, calling me by name and said, pointing to the other—'This is My Beloved Son. Hear Him!' " (Joseph Smith—History 1:17). Joseph learned by personal experience that the Father and the Son are two separate personages or individuals. Joseph taught that there are three persons who make up the Godhead and each person has his own being, identity, and personality. The three of them together are the one Godhead.

The Prophet Joseph increased our knowledge of God because he, like the prophets and apostles of old, saw and spoke with God face to face. God loves his children now as much as he did his children anciently, and so, for our benefit, he has called a prophet to lead us, just as he called Moses, Abraham, Isaiah, and the other ancient prophets. Joseph knew

God by talking to him, which is the best way to get to know a person. This is rather plainly stated in the Bible, but somewhere along the line this doctrine got mixed up and misunderstood. Let us see how the Bible describes God.

The first time God is mentioned in the Bible is in Genesis 1:1. The word here translated as God is the Hebrew word *Elohim*. Elohim is plural. It means more than one. The word for God is actually *El*. Just as we add "s" to a word to make it mean more than one, the Hebrew language adds "im." Thus *Elohim* should be translated *Gods*. The first verse in the Bible tells us that there was more than one God that created the earth. Even Paul says that God created all things by Jesus Christ (Ephesians 3:9). The Father and the Son were working together to create the earth. God says a little later, "The man is become as one of *us,* to know good and evil" (Genesis 3:22; emphasis added)? Doesn't the "us" mean the Father speaking to the Son, or perhaps the Son speaking to the Father? Clearly they are two individuals.

The word Elohim should be translated as Gods or Godhead. Thus the Godhead created the heaven and the earth. The Father, the Son, and the Holy Spirit are all members of the Godhead. Just as a school board is one organization with several members, so the Godhead is one organization with three members. The Godhead is the governing board of Gods.

Jesus Is the Son of God.

"Being in the form of God, [Jesus] thought it not robbery to be equal with God" (Philippians 2:6). That is, he was a full member of the board of the Gods or Godhead. The creeds would have us believe that Jesus is his own father. Unless God divides himself like an amoeba, which I do not think happens, he must have a father separate from himself. I do not know of anything other than single cells, like germs and amoebas, that can be their own father or mother.

What do other scriptures say about the Godhead? Jesus said, "I and my Father and I are one" (John 10:30). They must therefore be the same individual. He also said, "My Father is greater than I" (John 14:28). Therefore they must be two individuals. How can both these ideas be correct? We can't ignore either one, for they are both scripture. Could it be that when he speaks of the Father and himself being one Jesus means they are both on the one board of the Gods or members of the one Godhead.

Perhaps the writings of John will make this plainer. In John 17, Jesus prays to the Father for his disciples. In verse 11, he prays for the Twelve Apostles asking "that they may be one, as we are." Are the Twelve Apostles then going to become one individual without "confounding the persons or dividing the substance" as the Athanasian Creed says? Or is it more likely that they will become a group or quorum with twelve members, just as the Godhead is a group or quorum of three members? This makes more sense to me.

In verse 22, we find that all those who believe in the words of the apostles are to "be one, even as we are one." Now, are all believers to be stuck together in one body or are they merely each to become a member of the body of Christ, that is, the Church? It makes more sense to me that all the members will be in one body, the Church, and the apostles will be in one body, the Quorum of the Twelve Apostles, and that the Father, Son, and Holy Ghost will be in the one body—the Godhead or the Elohim. This is what the Prophet Joseph Smith taught, and thus he has increased our knowledge of God, even though Joseph's doctrines should have already been plain to anyone who read the Bible.

Man's Relationship to God

Now it has been shown that Jesus was a member of the Godhead. As the Apostle Paul says, "For in him dwelleth all the fulness of the Godhead bodily" (Colossians 2:9). He is authorized to speak for the other members of the Godhead. They all work together and the will of one is the will of the others.

Not only was Jesus a member of the Godhead, but he was also a man. As the Apostle Paul says, "For there is one God, and one mediator between God and men, the man, Christ Jesus" (1 Timothy 2:5). Paul said Jesus was a man. He was the Son of God in the spirit and in the flesh. We are the children of God in the spirit, though we are born of other parents in the flesh. Since we are all children of God and Christ is the Son of God, then Jesus is our brother, not just figuratively, but literally—you could even say "genetically"—as spirit beings.

The Apostle Paul spoke of this also. In explaining the Godhead, he says, "For we are also his offspring. Forasmuch then as we are the offspring of God, we ought not to think that the Godhead is like unto gold, or silver, or stone, graven by art and man's device" (Acts 17:28–29). Paul is explaining that God is not a statue made by men, but literally the father of all the people on Earth—the father of their spirits. If God is our father, then we have a genetic inheritance from him. When Moses says that man is made in the image of God, he says exactly what he means. Children are made in the image of their parents. We know we are not the offspring of God physically, therefore we must be the spiritual offspring of God. We were born to God as his spirit children.

This means that we are of the same race or species as God and Christ. We are of the race of the gods. Did not God say to Christ after the Fall that the man had become as the gods, to know good and evil? Being of the race of the gods, it is natural that we have the potential of being like our Father in Heaven. Matthew says, "Be ye therefore perfect, even as your Father which is in heaven is perfect" (Matthew 5:48). Perhaps we will not be members of the Godhead or the twelve apostles—for those positions are already filled—but junior gods, as it were who help bring about God's purposes on the earth and later in heaven.

We are told, "For though there be that are called gods, whether in heaven or in earth, (as there be gods many, and lords many,) But to us there is but one God, the Father" (1 Corinthians 8:5–6). Though there are others that are called gods there is only one God that we worship, and that is God the Father, the Father of our spirits. Others may help him, but if they are not of the Godhead they are not to be worshipped. So as the children of God, we may become junior gods by developing the abilities we have inherited from him.

It says in the scriptures that God is our father, but no one believed it until Joseph Smith showed how it was so for our spirits. The Bible says there are three in the Godhead, but no one understood this doctrine until Joseph made it plain. We should be thankful to the Prophet Joseph Smith for bringing us back to the teachings of the Bible concerning God and moving us away from the creeds of uninspired men.

Notes

1. George Charles Herbermann, *The Catholic Encyclopedia: An International Work of Reference on the Constitution, Doctrine, Discipline, and History of the Catholic Church* (New York: Encyclopedia Press, 1913), 2:33–34.

25

Extending Priesthood Authority

A number of years ago I had a friend—or perhaps I should call him an *acquaintance*—who found a book issued by an insurance company. It was a book of forms for the agent to fill out when people wanted to get insurance. He took this book and began selling insurance policies. He was making money. The problem was, he hadn't been hired, and the company didn't know he was selling policies. When some of the people he had sold policies to made claims on the insurance company, the company refused to pay the claim. Needless to say, he was in trouble with the law for doing this. Apparently he thought that all you needed to do was fill out the paperwork and do what the book said. But he was wrong. The company had not given him the authority to sell policies for them.

Many people pick up the Bible and start preaching from it, declaring that they have the means of helping others to gain salvation. They baptize people and administer the Lord's supper. They take contributions from people and start making money. The question is, have they been hired by "the company"? Does having the Bible give them the authority to preach and administer in the gospel? Having the insurance book did not give my friend the authority to sell policies. He knew how to fill out the paperwork, but he had not been hired. Having the Bible does not give ministers the right to preach, administer baptism or the Lord's supper, or take donations. They must be authorized by God to work for him, or he will not recognize what they do as valid and binding.

Can Men Get Their Religious Authority from Debate?

When the apostles were on the earth anciently, they had the authority from Christ to run his Church and to ordain others to do the work of the Church. God had put them in charge, or hired them. They did not get their authority from the scriptures. The New Testament did not even exist then. And the writings that became the Old Testament had not been compiled into one book. They got their authority from Christ. When the apostles were all killed, the bishops and others that had been ordained by the apostles continued the work.

A few hundred years went by, and things changed. The Roman emperor Constantine took over the directing of the church. He called a counsel of bishops and told them what to do. Did Constantine have the authority to tell bishops what to do? I do not think so. He wasn't even a member of the Church. As an emperor, his authority was of an earthly kind. Where did he get the authority to call and direct Church counsels? Not from the Lord, I am sure.

When the bishops met in counsel to decide on the doctrines of the church (doctrines which had already been decided by the apostles, by the way) they resorted to debate to try and settle their questions. They would argue about it, and the answer that sounded best or was the most logical according to the Greek philosophical system was then considered doctrine. This is not the way doctrine was established when the apostles were alive. Apostles prayed to God and got the answers to their questions by revelation. Debate does not give authority to pronounce doctrine.

Does Voting Give Man God's Authority?

Another way that men get authority over others is by voting. In the United States, as an almost-democracy (actually we are a democratic republic), we elect our public officials by voting for them. The one with the most votes gets the job. Does having the most votes or having the largest following mean you are chosen by God to run things for him? Many churches choose their ministers by having the members—or sometimes just the elders—vote on who they want for their minister and the one with the most votes is the winner. He gets the job.

If we look at the Old Testament story of Noah, we find that the only ones who voted for Noah were his wife, his three sons, and their wives. Everyone else laughed at Noah for building a big boat on dry ground.

Noah did not get the most votes, but he was a prophet and he was on God's side. Perhaps we should find out who God will vote for and go with his choice.

Another example is when Elijah held his contest with 450 of the priests of Baal. Elijah was just one man, and he was lined up against the king and 450 other men. If voting had been used to decide the issue, then Elijah would have lost. But Elijah won the contest, and all the other men were killed as a result (see 1 Kings 18). God alone voted for Elijah.

Men do not get authority from God by having others vote for them. God calls whom he will to be his representatives. Moses and Jonah did not ask for the job; indeed, they tried to get out of it. Samuel was but a little child when the Lord called him. No one voted for these men, but God wanted them and gave them his authority to do his work. We cannot just vote on whom we want to be a prophet. God will call whomsoever he will. It is then up to us to find out whom the Lord has chosen and to support the Lord's choice.

Can Men Get Authority by Force?

Most of the nations and kingdoms on the earth at this time are here because men went to war and the strongest leader—the one who could get the most support—became the king, dictator, or president. These men have power over the lives of the people in their nation. They can make laws according to their whim. They can run things as they like. Does having authority in national and governmental matters give a person authority in spiritual things?

Saul was the king of Israel. He was preparing for war with a neighboring state. The prophet Samuel had told him to wait until Samuel got there, so they could then offer sacrifice together, in the hopes that the Lord would be on their side in the coming battle. Samuel was late and, as Saul put it, Saul "forced himself" and offered the sacrifice that only someone having the priesthood should have done. When Samuel arrived and saw what Saul had done, Samuel pronounced a prophecy against Saul that the kingship would be taken from him (1 Samuel 13:7–14). Saul was the king, but that did not give Saul authority to offer sacrifices. Only priesthood holders were allowed to do that. Having earthly authority is not the same as having heavenly authority or priesthood. Saul was cursed for believing that he, as a king, had greater power than the prophet.

How Does God Give Authority?

The Prophet Joseph Smith records the coming of John the Baptist to give to him and Oliver Cowdrey the authority to baptize. John was the one who baptized Jesus, thus we know he had the authority from God to baptize. Joseph said that while they were praying, a "messenger from heaven descended in a cloud of light" and laid his hands upon them and ordained them saying, "Upon you my fellow servants . . . I confer the priesthood of Aaron, which holds the keys . . . of baptism by immersion for the remission of sins" (D&C 13:1).[1] Joseph did not just start baptizing on his own; he was ordained by the laying on of hands of one who already had the authority to baptize.

Later, Peter, James, and John—three of the apostles of Jesus—came to Joseph and Oliver and ordained them to be elders, just as they had done for Matthias in the New Testament (see Acts 1:23–26). Jesus is called a priest after the order of Melchizedek. Melchizedek held the priesthood power in the days of Abraham. Jesus gave this same priesthood to his apostles so that they could do the work of the Church. They had the same order of priesthood as Melchizedek. When Peter, James, and John gave Joseph Smith and Oliver Cowdrey this priesthood, Joseph and Oliver became priests after the order of Melchizedek. Joseph then had the authority to preach the gospel and run the Church, not by any authority of man, but from Jesus Christ, for Peter, James, and John got their authority from Jesus.

This is how Joseph said he received authority from God. He was hired by the company, or called by God, to do the things he did. He did not depend on force, his fast talking, the Bible, or the support of his followers for his authority; he got it from messengers of God.

If we look in the Bible to see how authority was given, we will find the same pattern. In the book of Numbers, we find that at the end of Moses's ministry, shortly before he was taken, he appointed Joshua to take his place as the leader of Israel. "And the Lord said unto Moses, Take thee Joshua the son of Nun, a man in whom is the spirit, and lay thine hand upon him; And set him before Eleazar the priest, and before all the congregation; and give him a charge in their sight" (Numbers 27:18–19). Authority was passed from Moses to Joshua, and it was done by the laying on of hands. Not only that, but the Lord told Moses who was to take his place. Joshua did not choose to become the next leader, nor did Moses choose Joshua. The Lord chose Joshua to be the prophet. Joseph Smith said that authority is given by the laying on of hands under the direction of the Lord, and the Old Testament agrees.

In the Acts, we read a good bit about the ministry of Paul the Apostle. How did Paul get authority to preach the gospel? In an account of a meeting of Church leaders at Antioch, we find this: "As they ministered to the Lord, and fasted, the Holy Ghost said, Separate me Barnabus and Saul [Paul] for the work whereunto I have called them. And when they had fasted and prayed, *and laid their hands on them,* they sent them away" (Acts 13:2–3; emphasis added). Here in the New Testament, we find the same pattern. Paul did not call himself to be a preacher; the Holy Ghost spoke through the leading brethren as to who should be missionaries. Then those missionaries were ordained by the laying on of hands before beginning their ministry. This is the way Joseph Smith said his ordination happened. He did not ask to be the head of a church, the Lord chose him. He did not start work until he had authority given him by the laying on of hands. This is the same pattern we find in the scriptures.

There are those who would have us believe that anyone who believes Jesus Christ is the son of God and Savior of the world has priesthood authority. Why then did Joshua and Paul have to be ordained by the laying on of hands before they began to work for the Lord? Priesthood authority to work for God must be given by one who already has that authority. I cannot give authority to someone else that I do not have myself. Joshua could not have been ordained by Caleb, for Caleb did not have the authority Moses did. Paul could not have been ordained an Apostle by Timothy, for Timothy did not have that authority himself.

To say you have priesthood authority without the laying on of hands by someone with that authority is to assume power you do not have. If you do this, the Lord will not recognize that you have authority. He has not hired you. The Prophet Joseph Smith said, "We believe that a man must be called of God, by prophecy, and by the laying on of hands by those who are in authority, to preach the Gospel and administer in the ordinances thereof" (Article of Faith 5).

How Has Priesthood Authority Been Extended over Time?

Now we come to the real reason for this chapter. What have Joseph Smith and his followers done to extend the priesthood? Who has the priesthood now? Let us begin by looking at the history of who had the priesthood in ancient times.

In olden times the patriarchs were the ones who held the priesthood. Melchizedek, Abraham, Isaac, and Jacob, are prime examples of ancient patriarchs. Apparently, the priesthood was limited to these patriarchs and was not given generally to their followers. Back then, the priesthood was not spread around very much.

With the coming of Moses, the priesthood was extended to the tribe of Levi, one of the twelve tribes of Israel. So about one-twelfth of the Israelites had the priesthood. At the time of Christ, the priesthood was given to all worthy Israelites. The Gentiles also could be ordained to the priesthood. This was a much wider base than just one of the tribes of Israel. The priesthood was spreading.

Now, in our day, the prophet Spencer W. Kimball, a successor to Joseph Smith, declared, "Every faithful, worthy man in the church may receive the holy priesthood, with power to exercise its divine authority" (Official Declaration 2). Now the priesthood can be given to every man on Earth—if they will believe, be baptized, and be worthy of it. Thus has the work begun by Joseph Smith extended the priesthood to every man.

I should mention here that every man in the Church who receives the priesthood is able to trace his priesthood by the laying on of hands, man to man, back to Jesus Christ. Thus, each man is assured that he really has the priesthood and that he hasn't received it because someone just decided to ordain others without having been ordained himself. The Catholic church traces its line of priesthood back to the Apostle Peter. All other Christian churches are off-shoots from the Catholic church or off-shoots of off-shoots of the Catholic church. I do not believe the Catholic church would have given reformers—or heretics, as the Catholic church called them—the priesthood power to organize a different church. Heretics were usually excommunicated, and sometimes even burned at the stake.

The priesthood is the authority "to administer in spiritual things" (D&C 107:8) and the power to bind on Earth and have it be bound in heaven (D&C 128:8). This is the authority Jesus gave to Peter the Apostle. This is the authority found in the Church of Jesus Christ of Latter-day Saints, restored by the Prophet Joseph Smith. Every man in the Church may be ordained to the priesthood if he is worthy. Thus we see the priesthood has spread over time from a few patriarchs to all the worthy men in the Church.

Notes

1. See also Peter George Mode, *Source Book and Bibliographical Guide for American Church History* (Menasha, WI: George Banta Publishing, 1921), 497.

26

Extending Scriptures

What Is Scripture?

We can begin by saying that scripture comes from prophets (see Romans 16:26). The Old Testament is divided into three sections, the Law, written by Moses; the prophets, written by various prophets in Israel; and the writings, or poetical books, again written by inspired men. In each case, the books are inspired by the Lord (except perhaps for the Song of Solomon). A prophet does not come up with his own revelation to give to the people; he waits for the Lord to tell him what to say. When the words of the Lord are delivered through his prophets, we have scripture.

The prophet Moses wrote the first five books of the Old Testament. Speaking of the things he wrote, he said, "Ye shall not add unto the word which I command you, neither shall ye diminish ought from it, that ye may keep the commandments of the Lord your God which I command you" (Deuteronomy 4:2). This would seem to indicate that the canon of scripture was closed, or that no more scripture was to be given after the first five books of Moses. If this were so, then we would have to throw away the rest of the Old Testament and all the New Testament. I do not think this is what Moses meant. Moses finished his books and did not want anyone messing with them. He did not want anything added to or taken away from *his books*. This does not mean that the Lord could not call another prophet to bring other scriptures to God's children. Subsequent prophets were told to write their own books, but they were not supposed to change what Moses wrote.

Jeremiah was a prophet in Israel shortly before the kingdom of Judah was taken captive. As a prophet, he wrote a prophecy of the bad things that were to happen to the kingdom of Judah. When this writing was read to the king, the king was angry and burned the scroll. When Jeremiah heard of this, he took another scroll and had Baruck, his scribe, write again what was in the scroll "and there were added besides unto them many like words" (Jeremiah 36:32). Jeremiah not only wrote the words of the prophecy again, but because he was a prophet, he was able to add many similar words to the book. Prophets write scripture.

When Jesus began his ministry, he taught the people many things. For about three years, he preached the gospel and worked with the people. In the Bible, we have his Sermon on the Mount, given at the beginning of his ministry, and a few stories of the miraculous things he did but not very much else until the last week of his life. Where is the record of all that Jesus did and taught during the years of his ministry? Wouldn't this have to be considered scripture also? If the word of the Lord is scripture, and Jesus, as the Lord, was teaching the people, then what he said should be scripture. Wouldn't it be nice to have his other teachings?

If what Jesus said was scripture, then not all that is scripture is necessarily contained in the Bible. There may be other scriptures that were not recorded or that were lost or rejected when the Bible was put into a single book. We know about the apocryphal writings which are in Catholic Bibles, but seldom in the Protestant Bibles. We know of some writings that were once claimed as scripture, but were rejected by the compilers of the Bible. We know of the writings of the Dead Sea Scrolls and the Nag Hammadi Texts. These are all religious writings, but we are not sure if they are scripture.

Scripture is the word of the Lord given to men. Whether it is written down and canonized or whether it is simply spoken under the influence of the Holy Spirit, it is the same (see 2 Timothy 3:16). To be canonized simply means that a group of individuals all agree that what is written is the word of the Lord. Of course, others may not agree. Scripture, then, is the word of the Lord to men—whether canonized or not.

The Prophet Joseph Smith said, "Whatsoever [men] shall speak when moved upon by the Holy Ghost shall be scripture" (D&C 68:4). This is the same definition as given in the Bible, but some have tried to change it. Now many people say scripture is only what is in the Bible and nothing else. Both God and Christ have spoken many things that are not in the Bible. Do these things not have the weight of scripture? Why should having a group of men agree that the part of the word of God that is recorded in the Bible is scripture exclude everything else? I do not think it does. Men do not have the intelligence to write or even to determine what scripture is. God determines what scripture is by saying it himself, through Christ, or by his Holy Spirit through his prophets. The canonizing of one book does not mean prophets have not written other books containing the word of God.

We are told to live by every word of God (Matthew 4:4). If we only live by what is in the Bible and ignore other words God has spoken to us through the Holy Spirit, then we are not living by every word of God. God has said much more than just what is in the Bible. On the day of Pentecost, when the apostles received the Holy Spirit, which sat on them like "cloven tongues of fire," they taught the people the things of God. Wouldn't it be nice to have the words they spoke to the people there? How can we live by them if we do not have them? I think the answer is that we need the Holy Spirit within us so that we can know the things of God. If we have the Holy Ghost with us constantly, then we can live by every word God gives us.

Now we seem to have come to a problem. If everyone who has the Holy Ghost can write scripture, won't this cause a lot of confusion? If we have the Bible, and ministers cannot even agree on what it says, and if everyone receives their own revelation, what hope is there that anyone will ever agree on the doctrine of Christ? People have been trying for over sixteen hundred years to agree on the truth in the Bible. Won't this just make for more confusion?

One thing that helps is that the Lord calls one man to be a prophet for all the people. The Lord called Moses to be the main prophet for all the Israelites. That way, the Israelites only had to believe that Moses was God's chosen Prophet in order for them to be on the right path. Moses, as the main prophet, was to judge all the other prophets to see that what they said was according to God's will. Moses wanted all his people to be prophets (see Numbers 11:29) so they could find out from the Lord that he was the head of the prophets. Regular members of the Church may prophesy, but their prophecy is subject to the head prophet (see 1 Corinthians 14:29–33).

For example, Aaron and Miriam complained against Moses because he had taken an Ethiopian for a wife. They said, "Hath the Lord indeed spoken only by Moses? hath he not spoken also by us?" Aaron and Miriam claimed to speak the words of the Lord. The Lord heard what they said and was displeased. The Lord said, "Hear now my words: If there be a prophet among you, I the Lord will make myself known unto him in a vision, and will speak unto him in a dream. My servant Moses is not so, who is faithful in all mine house. With him will I speak mouth to mouth, even apparently, and not in dark speeches; and the similitude of the Lord shall he behold: wherefore then were ye not afraid to speak against my servant Moses" (Numbers 12:2–8). After this, Miriam was leprous and had to be put out of the camp for seven days before she was cured. General prophets, like us, are subject to "The Prophet."

The Prophet Joseph Smith did not just see the Lord in a dream or vision (like watching TV) he was physically in the presence of the Lord. Therefore he was the one to straighten out doctrines that were not understood correctly. He could judge the other prophets and their words. This was how it was done in the days of Moses and in the days of the early Church, and it is how it is now done in our day. The Lord has one chief prophet on the earth at a time. This prophet is the President of the Church of Jesus Christ of Latter-day Saints. He is the prophet, seer, and revelator for all people on the earth. This is the Lord's way of maintaining order.

The prophet and apostles can receive revelation for the entire Church. Bishops can receive revelation for their individual congregation, but a bishop's revelation cannot contradict the words of the prophets and apostles. Members can receive revelation for themselves, but not for others. There is an order to how things are done. All can receive the revelation that Jesus is the Christ, that the canonized scriptures are true, or that the President of the Church is the true prophet. And each person can receive revelation about what he should do in his life, but he cannot get revelation for his bishop or anyone above himself or on an equal level in the line of authority. Individuals cannot receive revelation for the Church—only for themselves. Aaron and Miriam could not tell Moses what to do. We can't tell the bishop what to do, but the prophet can. Thus there is order in the Church and a way to judge if revelations are from God.

There is something else that should help keep things in order. Every person should get his information from the same source: God. Every person has the responsibility to be worthy of the Holy Spirit, so that he may know the truth. This is putting the responsibility to judge another's revelation on the individual, where it should be. The Lord knows this is not enough to keep things straight, which is why we listen to the prophet. Once we recognize who the prophet is and have it confirmed by revelation to us, then finding the truth becomes easier. When we have our own confirmation of who the prophet is, it becomes harder for us to go astray. Paul has said that the word of God is recognized by those who are spiritual or a prophet (1 Corinthians 14:37). If we are honest and ask in faith, we can have our own revelation of who the prophet is, along with a revelation of the truth of the prophet's words. We are encouraged by the prophets to get a witness from God of the things they say.

Have New Scriptures Been Given?

In September of 1823, the young Joseph Smith called upon God to ask for forgiveness and to know of his state and standing before God. While he was praying, a light appeared in his room and an angel came to him. The angel, named Moroni, told Joseph of a book written on metal plates and hidden in a hill not far from where Joseph lived. This book had been written by prophets among an ancient American people and was scripture. Joseph got the plates and translated the writings with the help of God. In the year 1829, Joseph published this book, which was known as the Book of Mormon. In true prophetic fashion, Joseph added scripture to the things that had been written by the prophets before him. This book was given to him by an angel, much like the law was given to Moses (Acts 7:53). The Book of Mormon was the first of Joseph's new books of scripture.

As Joseph Smith was doing the work the Lord had given him, he and the people who worked with him often had questions as to the doctrine of the Church and what the Lord would have them do. When these questions arose, the Prophet would inquire of the Lord to find out what the will of the Lord was. As the Lord spoke through him, Joseph would have a scribe write the things the Lord said. Over time, these writings became a good-sized collection. Joseph decided to publish these revelations, and thus came the Doctrine and Covenants. Again these words of the Lord were scripture.

When the Prophet Joseph was living in Nauvoo, a man brought some Egyptian mummies to display in the town. With the mummies were some scrolls. Some friends of Joseph bought the mummies and scrolls and gave them to him. Using the scrolls as his inspiration, Joseph wrote the Book of Abraham. Later, some other writings were included with it in a small book called the Pearl of Great Price. Thus we have more scripture coming from a modern prophet.

All these books—the Book of Mormon, the Doctrine and Covenants, and the Pearl of Great Price, as well as the Bible—have been canonized by the Church of Jesus Christ of Latter-day Saints as scripture. They are called the standard works of the Church. All these books have been joined together in a collection with common referencing, footnotes, indexes, and so on to make of them a single work. They have been added to the collection of scripture just as the writings in the Old Testament were added to the first five books of Moses, and the New Testament was added to the Old Testament to form the Bible. Even the name of the Book of Mormon has been changed to read, "The Book of Mormon: Another Testament of Jesus Christ."

Revelation to the prophets did not stop with the death of Joseph Smith. Successive presidents and prophets of the Church have continued to receive revelation from the Lord, and some of these revelations have been canonized and added to the words of the standard works or scripture of the Church. The Doctrine and Covenants has grown somewhat over the years as new information has been received from the Lord. Thus the work of the prophets has continued, and scripture has continued to come forth.

Why Would God Not Speak to Us Today?

There are those who claim that even though God spoke to Adam, Enoch, Abraham, Moses, Isaiah, Malachi, Jesus, his apostles, and many others, he no longer speaks to us. I wonder why that should be so. God spoke to men through prophets for the first four thousand years of Earth's history, and now we are told that there is nothing coming to Earth from the eternal realms. Let us see what some reasons for that could be.

Perhaps God has lost the power to speak to men. I do not believe this. God certainly has more power than we do, and we can speak to each other when we want to. Well then, perhaps God no longer loves us, so he ignores us. You must admit that as a people, we are a pretty sinful lot. If he got tired of our evil ways or being ignored, perhaps God decided to ignore us. This sounds like a possibility, but I do not believe God has stopped loving us. There are many good people on the earth as well as wicked. Even if God were to ignore the wicked, he would still work with the righteous, don't you think? God has told us to love each other, no matter what, so I think he would love us no matter what. He might be sad because of what we do, but he would still love us.

Could it be that we no longer need God? Perhaps we are such a righteous people that we can get along without him. But there are both righteous and wicked people on the earth now. Even if the righteous did not need him, God would still be working with the wicked to try to bring them to salvation. This theory does not work either.

One reason I have been told we no longer need God is because we have the Bible. According to some, the Bible has everything we need in it for our salvation. We need nothing else. I must take exception to this. If salvation is found in the Bible, then what was Jesus for? If salvation is found solely in the Bible, then was no one saved until about four hundred years after Christ, when the Bible was compiled? Jesus said, "Search the scriptures; for in them ye think ye have eternal life: and they are they which testify of me" (John 5:39). The Jews turned the worship of God into the worship of a book, the Old Testament. Jesus told them to search the scriptures because the scriptures testify of Christ. The Jews thought that in the scriptures they had eternal life, but this was not so. It was in Christ that they had eternal life. Now we find Christians doing the same thing the Jews did anciently. They worship the book that testifies of Christ instead of Christ himself. The Jews were called "the people of the book" because they had the Old Testament. Christians could just as easily be called "the people of the book" because they have the Bible. The Old Testament did not save the Jews, and the Bible will not save Christians. Christ will.

There are things the Bible does not tell us. For example, how are baptisms to be done? Today we have sprinkling, pouring, dipping, and immersing all done as baptisms. Are infants to be baptized, and, if not, at what age should baptisms start? Or are people simply baptized whenever they want to be? Should baptisms be done in a river as John and the apostles did them, or a lake, or a font built for that purpose? God has told us to be baptized and has said that it is necessary for salvation, yet in the Bible we cannot find even simple things like whom, when, how, or where a baptism should be done. Perhaps it does not matter, but perhaps it does. The Bible simply does not tell us.

If the Bible is all that we need, then why are there a thousand or more Christian churches, all teaching different things? We've had about sixteen hundred years to agree on the Bible, but we don't. I think we need some help from God and Christ. Wouldn't it be nice to know there was again a prophet on the earth who could explain what the Bible says and tell us what was left out of that book? I think that would be wonderful.

In the Book of Mormon, we learn that if we are without revelation, it is because of unbelief (Moroni 10:24). Many churches have said there was no longer revelation from heaven because we have the Bible and need nothing else. I suspect that because they have no revelation, they give this as an excuse. For many years, churches taught that there were no revelations from God except what was in the Bible, but now they are changing their minds. As the need for answers to basic questions becomes plain, and as no agreement can be reached on what is in the Bible, people are beginning to see the need for revelation from God through a prophet. Of course, they can't make themselves into prophets. God decides who his prophets will be. We should be looking for the prophet God has chosen.

27

Extending Gospel Ordinances

Baptism

Baptism is an ordinance of the gospel that was preformed by Jesus and the Apostles, as recorded in the New Testament. Most Christian churches follow this practice, though they have different ways in which they do it. The Bible quotes Jesus as saying, "Except a man be born of water . . . he cannot enter the kingdom of God" (John 3:5). Therefore it seems that if a person is not baptized, he will not go to heaven. The Prophet Joseph agreed with this. He said, "We believe that the first . . . ordinances of the Gospel are . . . Baptism by immersion for the remission of sins; [and] the laying on of hands for the gift of the Holy Ghost" (Fourth Article of Faith). Baptism is a necessary part of the gospel and is needed to get into the kingdom of heaven.

Some people have the idea that baptism was a new ordinance, established by John the Baptist, since the word "baptism" is not found in the Old Testament. But if baptism is needed for salvation, and no one was baptized until John started baptizing, then even the prophets who wrote the Old Testament are in trouble and can't be saved. The truth is that baptism was a standard practice for Jews long before the time of John the Baptist.

We read about Jews going to John to be baptized of him (Matthew 3:5–6). If baptism was something that John started and not part of the Law of Moses the Jews followed, why would they go to John to be baptized? Would they not rather have said, "Why is that crazy man taking his followers swimming?" The Jews recognized and desired baptism from John, a holder of the priesthood of Aaron, for their law required baptism.

In the Old Testament, the word for *baptism* is "washing." In the temple at Jerusalem, one of the objects in the temple was the "molten sea" (1 Kings 7:23). This was a big tub about fifteen feet across. Its purpose, we are told, was as a place "for the priests to wash in" (2 Chronicles 4:6). That is, the priests would wash or baptize the people there, for only the priests had authority from God to baptize. In other words, this was a place for baptisms. There were other buckets—or lavers, as they were called—for the priests to wash the sacrifices in (see 1 Kings 7:30). All who lived before the time of Christ are not doomed, for baptism was practiced before the time of Christ. Baptism is a part of the eternal gospel to which the Law of Moses was added.

Even if baptism did happen in Old Testament times, there is still a problem that the Christian world pretty much ignores because they don't know what to do about it. There have been billions of people who have lived and died on the earth without ever hearing about Jesus Christ. Many of these were good people, who lived their lives as well as they knew how. Are these people doomed because they were born in a time and place where they could not hear the gospel? That does not seem fair. Would it be fair of God to send one man to heaven because he was born into a Christian home and another to hell because he was born in a pagan home where he would not hear the gospel? This would make God unfair.

The story is told of an old German king, who was being taught by Christian missionaries during the decline of the Roman Empire. The missionaries told the old king that if he were baptized, he would be saved in heaven. He liked that idea, but then he asked about his parents and forefathers. He asked if they would be saved too. The king was told that his ancestors were going to hell, for they had not been baptized. The old king thought about this and then decided he would rather be in hell with his family than in heaven without them. Joseph Smith would have told him a different story about the fate of his ancestors.

What has Joseph Smith added to our knowledge of baptism? In 1 Corinthians 15:29 we find the statement, "Else what shall they do which are baptized for the dead, if the dead rise not at all? why are they then baptized for the dead?" I have been told that this refers to the spiritually dead who come to spiritual life as they are baptized. However, this does not agree with the context. Paul was speaking of the resurrection of the body when he was spoke of baptism for the dead. This means he was talking about those who were physically dead and who would be physically resurrected. This baptism was for those who were physically dead.

Joseph Smith brought back the practice of baptism for the dead that the Apostle Paul spoke about. This does not mean you dig up dead bodies and dunk them in water. That would be gross. It means you baptize a living person in the name of, or in behalf of, a person who is dead. The old German king could have been baptized for his dead ancestors, and thus they would have been given the same chance to go to heaven that he had.

The Apostle Peter said, "For this cause was the gospel preached also to them that are dead, that they might be judged according to men in the flesh, but live according to God in the spirit" (1 Peter 4:6). Why teach the gospel to the spirits of the dead, if they can't be baptized and go to heaven? Baptism for the dead gives everyone a chance to go to heaven, even if they have not heard the gospel while on Earth. The Prophet Joseph Smith extended the ordinance of baptism even beyond the grave.

The Lord Jesus gave Peter the power to seal on Earth and have it be sealed in heaven. Peter, James, and John gave this same power to Joseph Smith and Oliver Cowdrey. The power to seal on Earth and in heaven is still with the Church. Baptisms can be done by people here on Earth for the spirits of the dead and be effective in getting people into heaven after they are resurrected. The Lord authorized the Prophet Joseph to extend baptism to those who are dead. By doing this, God can be fair in his judgments.

Confirmation and the Holy Ghost

I can find no place in the Bible where confirmation is listed as an ordinance of the gospel. This seems to be another place where the Bible does not tell us all that we need to know about how to administer the gospel. There has, however, come down to us a tradition of confirmation by the laying on of hands after a person has been baptized. This tradition has been upheld by the Prophet Joseph Smith. He said, "And to confirm those who are baptized into the church, by the laying on of hands for the baptism of fire and the Holy Ghost" (D&C 20:41).

Baptism takes away the sins of the person because of their repentance and willingness to live a Christlike life. After his baptism, a person is then confirmed a member of the Church by the laying on of hands by the elders of the Church. This makes the person an official member of the

Church, or the body of Christ. The cleansing effect of baptism prepares a person to be worthy to become a member of the Church. Also, because the person is cleansed of his sins, he is fit to receive the Holy Ghost. The Holy Ghost will not reside in an unholy place; therefore, baptism prepares a person to be able to receive it.

After a person is baptized, his name should be recorded, so that he can be remembered and nourished with the good word of God (see Moroni 6:4). Sometimes when people sin, instead of coming to God and his representatives and repenting of the sin, they want to hide their sins. They do not feel worthy to go to church. They try to get themselves lost from the ministry of the Church. If their names are recorded, then they will be remembered, searched out, and invited back into fellowship with the Saints.

The Bible seems to be silent on confirmation, and some churches have done away with this gospel ordinance, but through a prophet, the Lord has brought this important part of the gospel back to us. Joseph Smith has added to our knowledge of confirmation and the receiving of the Holy Ghost as a gospel ordinance.

Sacrament of the Lord's Supper

There does not seem to be much to add about the sacrament of the Lord's Supper. The Apostle Paul gave some very plain instructions concerning it in 1 Corinthians 11:20–34. The Prophet Joseph simply agreed with this by saying, "It is expedient that the church meet together often to partake of bread and wine in the remembrance of the Lord Jesus" (D&C 20:75). The practice in the Church today is to administer the sacrament of the Lord's Supper almost every week during Sunday meetings. It is administered by those with priesthood authority, who have been authorized by God to do so.

Repentance

While not strictly an ordinance of the Church, repentance is expected of those who are followers of Christ. Over time, however, the original doctrine of repentance had been changed into penance. There is a difference. There was no such thing as penance in the ancient Church; the idea was added later. Now let us look at the two and see what the difference is.

J. Reuben Clark said, "To bring about the forgiveness of post-baptism sins, the dogma was developed that there must be acts of self-abasement or self-punishment called penance. . . . Men must pay for their sins,—not repent and forsake them." The priest fixed the penance and gave absolution. A person would atone through good works such as fasting, giving alms, praying, saying psalms, undergoing mortification, or participating in pilgrimages. Every sin had its penance assigned. Personal character was not involved.[1]

As you see from this, the person was expected to suffer for his own sins. The priest decided how bad that suffering should be. But I wonder, if the person must suffer for his own sins, what happened to the Atonement of Christ? Penance does not seem to use the Atonement wherein Christ suffered for the sins of mankind. If Christ has already suffered for our sins, why should we have to suffer for them also? I think repentance is a better philosophy.

In repenting, we must realize that we have sinned, feel sorry that we broke God's laws, confess that we have done wrong, try to fix the problem if we can, and never do the bad thing again. Finally, we must change our character to be more like Christ. The only suffering required is the sorrow we feel for having made God sad. We repent so we do not have to suffer because Christ did that for us already. The Prophet Joseph said that if we do not repent, we will suffer for our own sins, but if we do repent, Christ will do the suffering for us (D&C 19:4). With repentance, only those who will *not* repent have to suffer for their sins. Christ will suffer for those who repent. The Prophet Joseph brought back the true principle of repentance so that we may use the Atonement of Christ to pay for our sins and not have to suffer ourselves. He brought the power of the Atonement back to us.

Matrimony

I have attended a few weddings in my time. At a couple of them, I was even the best man. (But if I was the best man then why was the bride marrying the other guy? It's still a mystery to me!) I have noticed that when the couple is pronounced husband and wife, it is done by the authority of the state in which they live. The minister or justice of the peace says, "By the authority of the state of Tennessee, I now pronounce you man and wife." Where did the state of Tennessee get the authority to perform marriages? If I understand it right, marriage is a religious ordinance. The Constitution of the United States says congress is to make no law respecting religion. (I don't think they should make laws disrespecting religion either, but they do.) How, then, does Congress justify performing marriages, which are a religious ordinance? It seems someone has made a booboo.

The scriptures say, "What therefore God hath joined together, let not man put asunder" (Mark 10:9). Of course, if a couple is joined by the authority of the state of Tennessee, then God has not put them together—the government has. Even ministers announce that they are putting the man and wife together by the authority of the state. This means that God has not put them together, but the government has. The agreement is between the man, his wife, and the government. How do we get God back into marriage?

The Prophet Joseph explained that marriage should be done by priesthood authority, not just by the state. Also, God has revealed that if marriage is done by the proper priesthood authority it will last into the next life (see D&C 132:19). The Lord gave the Apostle Peter the sealing power to bind things on Earth and in heaven (see Matthew 16:19). Joseph Smith had this same power and could bind marriages together not just until death (the government can do that) but for the next world as well. Marriages in the temples of the Church of Jesus Christ of Latter-day Saints are not just performed by the authority of the government, but by the authority of the priesthood of God. Of course, the authority of the government is included when marriages are done in the temples. The United States government does not recognize priesthood authority any more than God recognizes the authority of the government in marriages. In the temples, authority from both are used to cover all the bases.

Thus we see that the Prophet Joseph extended marriage beyond the power of government to the power of God, and he extended marriage into eternity. Some people would find it hard to feel like they were in heaven if none of their family were there with them. Certainly the old king from Germany, whom I spoke of earlier, would have prefered to be in hell with his family than in heaven without them. Most people say that their families are the source of their greatest happiness in life. Wouldn't families be a source of great joy in the next life as well? There is greater joy when loving families are together, and God wants us to be happy.

Extreme Unction

There is an ordinance called extreme unction. This is given to a person when he is about to die. This ordinance is a comfort and a preparation to enter the realms of eternity. Extreme unction is administered by a priest to one in danger of death and includes both the application of oil to his organs of sense and the recital of prayers. "[It is] a spiritual medicine which diminishes the terrors of death, comforts the dying Christian, fortifies the soul in its final struggle, and purifies it for its passage from time to eternity."[2]

The Prophet Joseph approved of no such ordinance, but there is another that is quite similar. This is the ordinance of blessing the sick that they may regain their health. This is also spoken of in James 5:14–15: "Is any sick among you? let him call for the elders of the church; and let them pray over him, anointing him with oil in the name of the Lord: And the prayer of faith shall save the sick." This is not just for a person who is dying, but has been extended to the sick that thy might get well. I know of no place in scripture where extreme unction is performed. It must come down through tradition. The tradition must have started when the scriptural blessing of the sick, was performed without the healing power of God and subsequently changed to getting the person ready to die.

It is true that sometimes when giving a blessing to the sick, the elders anoint them with oil and then help prepare them for death in the words they say, but this is the exception. The blessing of the sick is usually to bring a person back to health. Joseph changed extreme unction back into a blessing of health for those who are sick, as the Bible tells us the ordinance should be done.

The Washing of Feet

There is one ordinance of the gospel that has not been extended by the Prophet; it seems to have actually been restricted. That is the ordinance of the washing of feet (see John 13:4–7). After supper, Jesus began to wash his Apostles' feet. This was the work of a servant, and Peter did not think the Savior should be doing such work. This was an act of humility and service on the part of the Savior. Jesus said, "He that is greatest among you shall be your servant" (Matthew 23:11). This was to show the apostles that they were not rulers like earthly kings, but truly servants to the people.

When he finished washing their feet, he said that just as he had washed their feet, they should wash one another's feet. When he said this, he made it an ordinance that should be administered in the Church. Thus the ordinance of the washing of feet came to be.

Today, there are several churches that practice this ordinance in the area where I live. The elders, the minister, and sometimes the members, get together and wash each other's feet. The Prophet Joseph, however, restricted who could participate in this ordinance. In the early days of the Church, there was an organization called the School of the Prophets. This ordinance of the washing of feet was how members were received into this school. Joseph said, "And ye shall not receive any among you into this school save he is clean from the blood of this generation; And he shall be received by the ordinance of the washing of feet, for unto this end was the ordinance of the washing of feet instituted. And again, the ordinance of washing feet is to be administered by the president, or presiding elder of the church" (D&C 88:138–40).

Now, the Presiding Elder of the Church is the prophet and President of the Church. He is the only one authorized to administer the ordinance of the washing of feet. The President of the Church, his two counselors, and the Twelve Apostles are all sustained in general conferences as prophets, seers, and revelators. It seems that these are the ones who are to take part in the ordinance of washing of feet when they take new members into their council. When the ordinance was given by Jesus, it was to his apostles, therefore—to the best of my knowledge—today the ordinance is reserved for the Quorum of the Twelve Apostles. Local elders and ministers are not to take part in this ordinance. (Unless the prophet directs otherwise.)

I can find no place in scripture where anyone but Jesus and the apostles took part in the ordinance of the washing of feet. Baptism and the Lord's Supper are mentioned as being preformed in the Church among the general membership, but the washing of feet is not. Therefore, it would seem that only apostles that are alive now are to take part in the ordinance. Here Joseph Smith made an ordinance more exact than what the modern churches get from the Bible.

Notes

1. J. Reuben Clark, *On the Way to Immortality and Eternal Life* (Salt Lake City: Deseret Book, 1949), 228–29.

2. James Cardinal Gibbons, *The Faith of Our Fathers: Being a Plain Exposition and Vindication of the Church Founded by Our Lord Jesus Christ* (London: John Murphy Company, 1905), 438, 441.

28

Extending Charity

From Alms to Welfare

In every age of the world, good people have taken it upon themselves to help the poor and needy. The giving of alms, as mentioned in the Bible, is a way every person can help those who are in need. This is something that anyone of any faith (or of no faith) can do. Anyone who has compassion for others can give alms when help is needed. Jesus commands his followers to do this. So what have the prophets of the Church of Jesus Christ of Latter-day Saints done to extend the ability to give alms and help the poor?

On the first Sunday of each month, everyone who is able is expected to fast and not eat anything for two consecutive meals. This allows a cleansing of the body and has been found to be healthy. Members then take the money that they would have spent on food for that day and donate it to the Church in order to help the poor. This money is used for no other purpose than to help the needy; there is no overhead. By fasting and donating that money, it really doesn't cost Church members anything, yet they are still helping the poor. This agrees in principle with what Isaiah said, "Is not this the fast that I have chosen? to loose the bands of wickedness, to undo the heavy burdens. . . . Is it not to deal thy bread to the hungry, and that thou bring the poor that are cast out to thy house? when thou seest the naked, that thou cover him" (Isaiah 58:6–7). People may give as their hearts move them, but the Church has organized the giving that the needy may be more easily helped.

The Church also has what are called bishops' storehouses. Food is put into these storehouses, and when someone has a need, he goes to the bishop and makes a request. If the bishop approves, the person then goes to the storehouse and takes what he needs. These storehouses are not only for Church members, but for others as well. When there is a natural disaster—such as a flood, hurricane, or earthquake—trucks are immediately loaded up from the storehouses and sent to the affected areas. Many times, the Church arrives with help before even the Red Cross can get there. Bishops and members of the priesthood often volunteer to help in the distribution of food, clothing, and medicine. The storehouses are able to do much good in this way.

The Church also runs farms where food is grown using volunteer workers. The food from these farms is then sent to the Church canneries where the food is processed and canned so it can be put into the storehouses. Using volunteer workers from the Church makes this more economical than buying the foodstuffs from regular markets. This also allows members to give of their time and energy to help the poor when they do not have an income that allows them to give very much money. I might mention here that when some members fast they give much more than the cost of food for one day.

I should also mention that there are people who come to the Church just because it has a way of caring for the needy. They think of Church welfare as being the same as government welfare. There is a difference. One of the guiding principles of our welfare system is that, "[Relief] is to be distributed for work or service rendered, [not as charity]."[1] This means that (except in emergencies) money is not just given to anyone who asks for it—the Church could go broke doing that. Instead, when people need help, they may be sent to work at the welfare farm or cannery. If there is no farm or cannery nearby, then they may be asked to help clean the local chapel or mow the chapel lawn. Sometimes members need work done at their homes, and those who need Church welfare do the work. The members then contribute to the fast offering fund, which is then given to the needy, who are doing the work. It is as it says in the Bible, "If any would not work, neither should he eat" (2 Thessalonians 3:10). The Church welfare system helps to abolish the dole and teaches people to be self-supporting. "The confirmed idler is not entitled to help."[2]

Humanitarian Aid

In the Church of Jesus Christ of Latter-day Saints, instead of passing around a plate for contributions, the members fill out a little slip of paper, stating how much they want to give for tithing, fast offerings, and other funds. One of the categories listed on this slip is humanitarian aid. Like the other kinds of donations, this is completely voluntary. The humanitarian aid fund not only helps in emergencies, but supports a number of ongoing programs to help the poor. There are wells being dug for clean water in South America. There are inoculation programs to stop the spread of disease in Africa. There is ongoing relief for refugees who have been forced out of their warring countries. These and many other programs are run by the Church to help those in need.

The Church also runs a system for job placement. In each congregation, there is a person who is given the task of finding work for the unemployed or better jobs for those who are employed but do not make enough money. This program is still struggling in some places, but the Church is working to make it better. There is also a perpetual education program to loan money to young people so they can go to school. In countries outside the United States, there are often no student loans or grants to help with tuition. The Church pays for school tuition and after they graduate, the students pay back the money. When the money is paid back, it then goes back into the fund to help someone else who wants to go to school. The same money may help another student about every four years.

Spiritual as Well as Physical Aid

There is another kind of aid that the Church is able to give, and that is spiritual aid. Like most churches, the Church of Jesus Christ of Latter-day Saints meets each week to instruct its members in their duties and in how to become like Christ. But the weekly meeting is just the beginning of the Church's help and support of its members.

There is a program in the Church called home teaching. The families of the congregation are divided up among elders of the Church, and the elders are expected to visit those members who are assigned to them to check on their welfare. When this program works correctly, every member of the congregation has a visit from a representative of the bishop each month. The elders encourage their assigned families to pray, attend church, and to be good. Often a short lesson is given. If the family is experiencing problems—whether spiritual, financial, or otherwise—then the Church can be told of these problems and help can then be given.

All males in the Church over the age of twelve may belong to a priesthood group or quorum. The women belong to the Relief Society, the Church's organization for women. Children belong to the Primary.

Anyone having problems can go to their quorum leader or to the bishop, so the resources of the Church can be brought to the aid of the member. Help is always there when a person needs it.

Notes

1. James R. Clark, *Messages of the First Presidency: 1935–1951* (Salt Lake City: Bookcraft, 1975), 6:11.
2. Clark, *Messages of the First Presidency*, 86.

29

Extending Faith

More Evidence to Build Faith

In court, the more evidence you have, the greater your chances of winning your case. In the Church of Jesus Christ of Latter-day Saints, the Lord has provided many things as evidence on which to base your faith.

The world in general has the Bible. There are also the Dead Sea Scrolls, the Nag Hammadi writings, the Lakish letters, and a number of other writings all supporting the history of the Bible. In the Church, there is also the Book of Mormon, which is the history of a colony from Jerusalem who came to America six hundred years before Christ. The Book of Mormon consists of the writings of the prophets among this group of people in America. Like the other newly found writings, it supports and explains what is found in the Bible. There is also the Doctrine and Covenants, which is the writings of Joseph Smith and his successors as the leaders of the Church. These writings support and extend the teachings of the Bible. The Pearl of Great Price is also recognized as scripture by the LDS Church. Here we have more of the word of God. That means we have more scripture on which to base our faith.

The Bible was written by prophets. Prophets are men whom God has chosen to be his representatives to the people of the earth. With the coming of Joseph Smith, a new line of prophets has been established by the Lord. Each of Joseph Smith's successors has been sustained and ordained as a prophet, seer, and revelator. This way, if the Lord has new information to give to the world, he always has a prophet through whom he can work. When God wanted to preserve a few people during the flood, he called a prophet—Noah—to build an ark. When the Hebrews had turned to false gods, the Lord called Abraham to leave his country and go to Canaan to preserve the worship of the true God in the world. When the Israelites were in bondage in Egypt, he called Moses to lead them out of Egypt to the promised land. Now, when there are many hundreds of churches all calling themselves Christian, the Lord has called new prophets to teach the people the correct way to worship him. With more true prophets, we have more support for our faith.

Moses once said, "Would God that all the Lord's people were prophets" (Numbers 11:29). John said, "The testimony of Jesus is the spirit of prophecy" (Revelation 19:10). All of the Lord's people need to have the testimony of Jesus. That is, they need to get a revelation from God that Jesus is the Christ, the Son of God. If they have a testimony of Jesus, then they are prophets, for the only way to get this testimony is for God to reveal it to you. This is another way the Lord increases our faith, by giving us the testimony of Jesus by the spirit of prophecy.

The prophets have increased our faith, giving us more to hope for. Christians tell us that if we are good and do what we should, then we will go to heaven. This sounds wonderful, but what is so great about heaven? What will we do there? What reward will we have? Why is heaven so wonderful?

We are told that heaven is wonderful because God is there. Being in the presence of God is a reward in itself. There we will sing in the choirs, praising and adoring God for all eternity. Well, I guess that is fine for some people, but what about those who can't sing very well? When I started college, I took a voice class to learn how to sing. After the first course ended, the teacher told me that I had two choices: I could take an F and try again next semester, or she would raise my grade to a D if I would promise not to take any more music classes. Now, with encouragement like that, it may be hard for me to sing for our Heavenly Father for all of eternity. If singing and harp playing is all there is to do in heaven, not everyone will be happy there.

The Prophet Joseph Smith told us a little more about heaven. In Doctrine and Covenants 76, he explains that there are three degrees or kingdoms of heaven. The highest, the celestial, is compared to the sun in glory; the middle, the terrestrial, is compared to the glory of the moon; and the lower, the telestial, is compared to the glory of the stars (D&C 76:70–89; see also 1 Corinthians 15:40–42). These are all parts of heaven for they are all kingdoms of glory. Now who goes to which kingdom?

To get to the lowest or telestial kingdom, there is but one requirement. A person must not deny the Holy Spirit. I think that on Judgment Day, when we stand before the bar of God, and the Holy Spirit tells us the truth of God and Jesus Christ, that there will not be many who will reject him. When the people are asked to accept either Christ or the devil as their king and ruler, I think that even those we would call wicked will be willing to say that they want to accept Christ as their king. Those who go to hell with the devil and his followers will be those who knowingly choose to go there after the Holy Ghost has told them the truth.

I do not think that God, who loves all his children beyond our ability to understand, would send any away who wanted to be in his kingdom. He might put them in the basement—that is, the telestial kingdom—but I think he would still want them in his house. So, even those who are quite wicked in this life have a place of glory as long as they do not reject the Holy Ghost and his testimony of Christ, for the Holy Ghost will have influence in the telestial kingdom.

We have been told that the telestial kingdom, the lowest of the kingdoms of glory, is so wonderful that if we knew what was there we would easily be willing to die just to get there. This is like the heaven of general Christianity, though there is more to do there than just sing all the time. If this lowest kingdom is so wonderful, what are the higher kingdoms like?

In the highest, or celestial, kingdom, where God the Father dwells, we are told that you will be able to have your family with you. When the Bible speaks of Isaac and Jacob being gathered to their ancestors, we believe this is a literal gathering (see Genesis 25:8, 17). Good and righteous men may live with their families after this life. To give up the love of a spouse after many years together on Earth does not seem right. With a proper priesthood sealing in the temple, families can be together again after this life. Those who are not sealed will be alone in the hereafter, just as many Christians teach.

In the celestial kingdom, there will be more to do than just singing with the choirs of heaven. There will be work to do, things to learn, and others that still need our help. We are commanded to become like God, but he will not just zap us by magic and make us like he is. We will still need to learn what he knows. This may take a while. We will still need to teach others the things we learn, just as mothers and fathers teach their children now. People say the greatest happiness is in the home with a loving family. In the celestial kingdom, there will be homes with loving families in them. This is where the greatest happiness is. If we cannot fit into a loving home, then we must go to a lesser kingdom where people are as the angels of God—simply individuals.

Being with the family you love in the celestial kingdom is an incentive to be good and will give you hope that will increase your faith. The greater the reward, the greater will be your hope and faith that you can obtain that reward.

The Assurance of a Testimony

The Jews are called the "people of the book" because they have the writings of the Old Testament prophets. They became so concentrated on the book that when the true writer of the book came, they did not recognize him. Christ gave a different interpretation of the scriptures than they were used to, so many Jews rejected him. In our time, Christians are so concerned with the Bible that when the Lord sends modern prophets to them, they reject them if the prophets do not agree with their interpretations of the Bible. The Christians have fallen into the same error the Jews did anciently.

We are not to worship a book. We are to worship God the Father, Jesus Christ, and the Holy Ghost. To do this correctly, we need to know what they are telling us to do now. This requires us to get a testimony; that is, we need to be able to get information from the Lord himself through the Holy Spirit. We cannot put our interpretation of the Bible above what the Lord says about it. Enoch was a great prophet, but if Noah had only read the words of Enoch, how would he have known he was to build the ark? Enoch never built an ark. Noah would have drowned in the flood if he had only read the words of Enoch and not listened to the Lord. We need to know what the Lord is saying to us now.

On an episode of the TV show *Touched by an Angel*, one of the characters, Monica, was about to be committed to an institution for saying she was an angel. She said, "Why is it that when you talk to God, you are praying, but when God talks to you, you're nuts?" Prayer is communication. If you talk to God and he does not talk back, that is not communication, and it is not real prayer. I do not think prayer would be very useful if God could not speak back. We might as well just memorize a few prayers and say them over and over by rote. But to speak to God and get information from him on what we should do, and what the truth is would be useful. It would also strengthen our faith. Latter-day Saints are expected to pray and get revelation for themselves from God. This increases their faith.

30

Extending the Atonement

The Atonement Extended to Cover Original Guilt

There was a boy at school where I work that was constantly getting into trouble. When anything was done, and we did not know who did it, we immediately suspected him. On one such occasion, we accused him, but he refused to acknowledge his guilt. It was only after a good bit of searching that we found out that he was not guilty after all. He was greatly saddened and frustrated that we found it hard to believe him.

Speaking of guilt, there are those who believe we have guilt thrust on us from the Fall of Adam. Certainly Adam and Eve introduced a knowledge of evil, pain, sickness, and death into the world, but did they also bring guilt? I am like the boy who we thought was guilty when he was not. Just as that boy was sad and frustrated that we accused him when he had not done it, so I am frustrated and sad because Adam was the one who ate the forbidden fruit, not me. Why should I have to feel guilty because of what he did? I have done a lot of other things I could feel guilty for, but eating of that fruit is not one of them. What can we say about this?

I think the first thing we have to consider is the purpose of the Atonement. The scriptures say, "As in Adam all die, even so in Christ shall all be made alive" (1 Corinthians 15:22). The purpose of the Atonement is to undo the bad part of what the Fall of Adam did. The Fall brought pain, sickness, and death. By the Resurrection of Christ, we too will be resurrected and no longer have pain, sickness, and death. It is true that the cure will take a while to take effect, but all of the effects of the Fall of Adam will eventually be overcome by the Atonement. We need not feel guilty about what Adam did because Christ is going to fix it.

The Prophet Joseph Smith has written, "The Son of God hath atoned for original guilt" (Moses 6:54). There is no guilt that comes to us from Adam; Christ has taken that away. There may, however, be guilt that comes to us from our own sins. Adam may have set up the conditions that brought us freedom to choose, but we choose to sin ourselves. Christ proved that we need not sin by coming to Earth himself and living a perfect life. The wonderful thing about the Atonement is that we can have our own sins remitted or taken away if we are willing to repent. Adam did not cause us to sin; he merely set up the situation so we can sin. Christ does not take away all our sins automatically, but he will take them away if we repent and change our evil ways. All the evil of the Fall can be done away in Christ, if we allow it to.

Some people blame Adam for all the evil in the world. If they do, they should also thank him for all the good in the world. Remember that the tree he ate from was the tree of the knowledge of *good* as well as the knowledge of evil. There would have been neither good nor evil without the Fall. There would have been existence, but existence without purpose. That is why the Fall was part of the plan from the beginning. Without the Fall, there would have been no good in the world.

Also, if you think about it, since Adam had no knowledge of good and evil or the effects thereof, just how much of a moral choice was it for him, eating the forbidden fruit? When Eve walked up saying "have some fruit," ir was the first time Adam had ever seen anyone disobey God. Adam had been told he would die, but he had never seen anyone or anything die. How could he know what death was? I think Adam should have as much right to repent as we do. Considering how God stacked the deck against him, I think it is the least God could do for him.

Salvation for Infants

The Bible teaches that for a man to be saved, he must be born of the water and of the spirit. In other words, we need to be baptized and receive the Holy Ghost (see John 3:5). Without baptism, there is no hope of salvation. In medieval times, this was taken to mean that little children needed to be baptized if they were to be saved. This is the natural result of the doctrine of original guilt. This meant that any little child who was not baptized and who died would automatically go to hell. Lately, the doctrine has been changed to have them go to a purgatory of mild torture instead of really bad torture. Still, this does not sit well with me.

Little children cannot request baptism. How could a fair God hold them responsible for what they had no control over? That would be like holding me responsible for what Adam did. That is not fair. Baptism is for repentance. Little babies cannot repent. They do not know anything about sin or repentance. I don't think that to cry when hungry or to mess a diaper is sinning.

In the Book of Mormon, we read, "Listen to the words of Christ, your Redeemer, your Lord and your God. Behold, I came into the world not to call the righteous but sinners to repentance; the whole need no physician, but they that are sick; wherefore, little children are whole, for they are not capable of committing sin; wherefore the curse of Adam is taken from them in me, that it hath no power over them" (Moroni 8:8). "And he that saith that little children need baptism denieth the mercies of Christ, and setteth at naught the Atonement of him and the power of his redemption" (Moroni 8:20). All of Moroni 8 speaks of the redemption of little children by the Atonement of Christ. Again, if the Atonement does not fix what the Fall of Adam caused, then what is it for? It would serve no purpose. But the Atonement does fix the Fall of Adam and little children are saved by the Atonement of Christ and do not need baptism, for they do not understand how to sin as we do. I would not want to be the one to deny the Atonement. If I deny salvation through the Atonement to infants, then Christ might deny the Atonement to me.

The Atonement Extended into the Spirit World

Christianity is being taught all over the world. There are now Christians in every country on Earth. The people are learning of Jesus and the things he did for the world. The gospel is being spread everywhere.

In many places, there are people who are the first in their families to hear the gospel. These people accept the gospel and look forward to heaven. But sometimes there is a great disappointment that comes with the gladness of the gospel. All of the parents, grandparents, and other ancestors of these people have never heard the gospel of Christ. According to most Christian teachings, all these people will go to hell. It does not seem right for a person who did the best he could with what he knew to go to hell. That would mean that he was punished for what other Christians failed to do. If Christians never got the gospel to a person before he died, then it would be the Christian's fault. One person should not be punished for what another did or failed to do. This is a problem that Christians do not seem able to answer well. Is there an answer? Yes!

The Apostle Peter said, "For for this cause was the gospel preached also to them that are dead, that they might be judged according to men in the flesh, but live according to God in the spirit" (1 Peter 4:6). How can the gospel be taught to the dead? Well, the dead are spirits. Spirits have knowledge and understanding, so all that would be necessary would be to go to where the spirits of the dead are. Peter said of this, "For Christ . . . being put to death in the flesh, but quickened by the Spirit: By which also he went and preached unto the spirits in prison" (1 Peter 3:18–19). Christ, as a spirit, crossed the great gulf that separated the righteous from the wicked in the world of spirits and began teaching the gospel to those who were in spiritual bondage. We are even told that he went specifically to the spirits of those who were disobedient in the days of Noah. Perhaps some lived so far away that they never heard Noah preach.

Thus we see that the gospel has been taught to the spirits of those who have died. This would serve no purpose unless they also were allowed to accept the gospel and come under the covenant of God. Therefore we must believe that God is fair after all and that the work that Christ began in teaching the spirits of the dead continues. There were many Old Testament prophets who testified of Christ while they were alive on Earth. Once Christ had bridged the gulf to the spirits in prison, these prophets could continue the work of giving them the gospel. I have spoken elsewhere about baptism for the dead. Thus we see that the dead may come under the covenant and be baptized and have the Atonement cover the sins they committed in life.

This means that those who died without hearing the gospel will hear it in the world of spirits. They will have the opportunity to be baptized and do everything else they need to do to obtain salvation in the highest heaven. In this way, the Atonement is made available to those who have ignorantly sinned (see Mosiah 3:11). Of course, they still have to obey the covenant to get that salvation. Judgment can only come after the covenant has been accepted if it is to be fair.

There is a warning I should give you here. You had better not say, "I will wait until the next life to accept the gospel because I am having too much fun to want to repent now." If you put it off here, you will probably put it off there. Your personality will not change. If you reject the gospel here, you may reject it there. I wouldn't take that chance.

So we see that the Atonement has been extended into the world of spirits. This must be so for God to be fair. Ignorance will be no excuse, for the gospel will eventually be taught to all—whether living or dead—and all will be judged according to what they do with what they know. That is fair.

The Atonement Is for All Living Things

It is by the Atonement of Christ that men are redeemed from death in the resurrection and saved from the devil by their repentance. Resurrection is a free gift given to all mankind. Are there other things that may be redeemed by the Atonement as well as mankind?

With the Fall of Adam, death came into the world. People are not the only things that die. Plants and animals also die. Every living thing has a soul or spirit within it (see Job 12:10). People have spirits within them that make them live. If animals and plants are alive, then it follows that they also have spirits within them that make them live. We are told that "as in Adam all die, even so in Christ shall all be made alive (1 Corinthians 15:22). This means that the Atonement not only covers men and women but also all the animals and even the plants that live on the earth.

There are people who love their pet dogs or cats almost as much as their children. To be the happiest in heaven, they would want these pets to be with them. If their pets are resurrected, then these people will enjoy being with them after they are resurrected. The Atonement works for everything that has a spirit or life within it.

31

Extending Salvation

Extending Salvation to Exaltation

Before we can talk about extending salvation, we must first decide just what salvation is. If someone is floating on a life raft in the middle of the ocean and a ship comes by and picks them up, we say the ship saved them. What were they saved from? The answer is death. Without help, they would either have starved to death or died of dehydration in a short time. In like manner, our salvation means we will be saved from death by the Atonement of Christ. Christ does this by bringing about the resurrection which will bring all people back to life. So salvation is being saved from death.

If you are a soldier and are captured by the enemy, and your friends come to rescue you from your captors, then you are saved from your enemy. In like manner, by our repentance and faith in the Atonement of Christ, we may be saved from our enemy, which is the devil. So salvation consists of two things. Being saved from death and being saved from the devil. This is Christian salvation. Now how could the Prophet Joseph extend this salvation?

To gain salvation from death and the devil, all that is needed is to accept Jesus Christ as your Savior. But the scriptures also tell us that we will be judged by our works (Revelation 20:12–13). If faith in Christ is all that is needed for salvation, how then are we judged by our works? The Prophet Joseph Smith said, "In the celestial glory there are three heavens or degrees" (D&C 131:1). In other words, even though all believers will go to heaven, and avoid both death and the devil, they will not all obtain the same reward. Some will receive greater rewards than others according to their works (Revelation 20:12; see also 1 Corinthians 15:40–41).

Salvation is free by the Atonement (see 2 Nephi 2:4), but exaltation—that is, to go to the highest heaven—must be earned by our works. Thus salvation or experiencing the glory of God is extended by the Prophet to three kingdoms of glory, the lowest kingdom being like the usual Christian heaven. Now let's look at the highest heaven.

Individual Salvation to Family Exaltation

In Matthew we read the following, "For in the resurrection they neither marry, nor are given in marriage, but are as the angels of God in heaven" (Matthew 22:30). Many people take this to mean that in heaven we are as the angels and have no families, and some teach that we will not even recognize those we knew on Earth. When the Prophet Joseph said we could be married here on Earth by the power of the priesthood and have the marriage last into the eternities, many Christians looked at this scripture and said he got this doctrine wrong. While many agreed that it would be nice to be with their spouse and children in the next life (for that is where they got their greatest joy in this life) this scripture says otherwise, and we must believe the scriptures. For these skeptics, ancient scriptures were more important than revelation from God now.

Does this mean we can only be angels in the next world? What about being a joint-heir with Christ (Romans 8:17)? I think Christ is more than just an angel, so if we are joint-heirs with him, we should be a little higher than the angels too. How do we answer this?

The answer is in the verse just before the one previously quoted. It says, "Jesus answered and said unto them, Ye do err, not knowing the scriptures, nor the power of God" (Matthew 22:29). Without the priesthood, the Jews could not be sealed together in marriage for the next world. The Jews did not understand the scriptures that taught about eternal marriage and they did not have the priesthood—or at least not the Melchizedek, or higher priesthood—by which these eternal marriages could be done. The Jews did not have the sealing power, but Peter did (Matthew 16:19). If Peter were to use the keys of the kingdom to bind marriages on Earth, they would be bound in heaven. So also those with the priesthood power today can bind husbands and wives together and they will be together in eternity. Without this power, we can only hope to be as the angels.

This is further explained in Hebrews: "But to which of the angels said he at any time, Sit on my right hand, until I make thine enemies thy footstool? Are they [the angels] not all ministering spirits, sent forth to minister for them who shall be heirs of salvation [exaltation]" (Hebrews 1:13–14). By this we see that those who have salvation—and here we believe this should be translated *exaltation*—will have the angels to minister for them, just as Christ has angels to minister for him. Thus those who are exalted are not angels but are equal heirs with Christ. This is what the scriptures say.

This is why people in the Church want their marriages to be done by the power of the priesthood, not just by the power of the state. Those married only by the power of the state will only be angels in eternity, while those married by the priesthood will be families in the next world. We will be a part of God's family. This is what Jesus meant when he said they would be as the angels of God in heaven because they knew not the power of God. If people declare the family to be the greatest source of happiness here on Earth, then wouldn't the family be the greatest source of happiness in the celestial world? I think so.

Appendix

Information about Prophets

In 1820, something happened in upstate New York that had not occurred for a long time. A young boy by the name of Joseph Smith saw a vision of God and Christ. He tells of reading in the Bible in James 1:5 where it says if you lack wisdom, ask of God. He did just that. He went into the woods to be alone and began to pray to God. In answer to his prayer, there was a great light that shined from heaven, and in that light Joseph saw a vision of God the Father and his son Jesus Christ (See Joseph Smith—History 1).

Having a vision from God would make Joseph Smith a prophet. There had been no prophets since about 100 AD. It had been so long that people had come to believe there were to be no more prophets. Rather than checking to see if he met the requirements of being a prophet, the people who lived near him chose to persecute him. They tried to get him to say he had not seen a vision from God. Just as the Apostle Paul had seen a vision and would not deny it, so Joseph Smith would not deny what he had seen. Perhaps now, almost two hundred years later, we will not do as they did and let our prejudice lead us, but will check to see if he fulfills the requirements of being a prophet.

When the Lord calls a prophet, what that prophet says, in the name of the Lord, will agree with the scriptures that are already given. Not only that, but every prophet also has the responsibility of going beyond what has already been given in scripture to further the word of the Lord. This does not mean he must agree with your own private interpretation of scripture, but he will extend the original meaning of that scripture. That is, a prophet is to add to the word of the Lord. That is how we got the scriptures in the first place. Prophets write the words of the Lord, each one adding to what has been given by former prophets.

Now, to see if Joseph Smith is a prophet, we need to do a couple of things. First, look in scripture to see if he meets the definition of what a prophet is. Then, since we lack wisdom, we should do as James directs—we should pray and ask the Lord if he truly is a prophet. Let us begin with a look at what prophets are and what they do. Let us see if Joseph Smith meets the scriptural criteria for being a prophet.

What Are Prophets?

Prophets are servants of the Lord (see 2 Kings 17:23). Let us look at Moses for an example. Moses was a Hebrew with an Egyptian upbringing. He then went to Midian and started herding sheep. It was there that the Lord called him to be a prophet, speaking to him from the burning bush. The Lord gave Moses a job to do. He was to deliver the children of Israel from Egypt. Moses became the Lord's servant, carrying out what the Lord wanted done. Moses did not decide what he would do, the Lord told him what to do. Moses was reluctant at first—he started making excuses and tried to get out of it. It was a hard thing the Lord required of him, but the Lord helped him, and he did it.

Joseph Smith was given the jobs of translating the Book of Mormon and organizing the Church. He did not come up with these tasks on his own; God commanded him. Indeed, he could not have done them on his own. Can you imagine a twenty-year-old with a third-grade education writing a one-thousand-year religious history and making it all fit together? I have tried some writing, and it isn't that easy. Just as God helped Moses to lead the Israelites from Egypt, he helped Joseph Smith to do the jobs he had been given.

The Lord chooses his prophets (see Amos 7:14–15). When Samuel was just a boy working in the temple under Eli, the Lord called him to be a prophet (see 1 Samuel 3). The Lord knew who he wanted for his prophet. The same was true for Saul in the New Testament. He was fighting against Christ, but when the Lord called and taught him the truth, he became Paul, a great supporter of the gospel, a great missionary, and an apostle. Now who would think of God calling a little boy like Samuel to be a prophet, or a great persecutor of the Church like Saul to be an apostle? The Lord will choose who he wants, not who we think he should. We can't tell the Lord who his prophets should be.

Joseph Smith was a poor farm boy. When he went into the woods to pray, he did not go with the idea of becoming a prophet. He just wanted to know which church he should join and what the truth was. Then God spoke to him and told him what he was to do. Joseph did not choose himself, he was chosen by God for the work God wanted done.

The scriptures tell us, "Surely the Lord God will do nothing, but he revealeth his secret unto his servants the prophets" (Amos 3:7). Apparently this is the way the Lord works on Earth. When he has a work to do for the children of men, he chooses a prophet and tells the prophet his secret—that secret being the gospel of Jesus Christ. God then tells his prophet what the prophet is to do to make the gospel work. God will not do anything without a prophet through whom he teaches the people. He will not teach the gospel, establish and run a church, or provide salvation to his children without working through his prophets. If God will do nothing without his prophets it is important to find out if Joseph Smith was indeed a prophet.

How to Recognize a True Prophet

A true prophet will be a witness of Jesus Christ and his Atonement (see Acts 10:43). In the New Testament, all the books are about Christ, what he did, and how we can live the gospel as he taught it. The goal of Christians is salvation. Without knowing about Christ and the Atonement, how can we be saved? Paul was a witness of Jesus Christ, even though his witness came after the Lord's death and Resurrection. Now let us see how Joseph Smith was a witness of Jesus Christ.

In 1829, Joseph Smith published a book called the Book of Mormon. This is where the nickname "Mormon" comes from. (The actual name of the Church that was started by Joseph Smith is the Church of Jesus Christ of Latter-day Saints.) More recently, this book has been officially titled, "The Book of Mormon, Another Testament of Jesus Christ." On the title page of the Book of Mormon we find it was written "to convince Jew and gentile that Jesus is the Christ." The Old Testament is a testimony to the people that the Messiah would come and contains many prophecies about him. The New Testament tells of Christ and how he fulfilled the prophecies given about him in the Old Testament. The Book of Mormon testifies of Christ and his work among the people of the Americas. It is as much a witness of Christ as the Bible is. Joseph Smith, then, fulfills this requirement for being a prophet, for he testifies of Christ.

A prophet will not ask you to follow other gods (see Deuteronomy 13:1–3). The children of Israel were told to follow the God of Abraham, Isaac, and Jacob. In the New Testament, the Jews were told to follow Christ as the Son of God because he would follow his Father's will perfectly.

Joseph Smith told his followers to follow the God described in the Bible—the God of Abraham, Isaac, and Jacob. Joseph did not agree with the creeds of Christendom that define God as indefinable, immaterial, and incomprehensible, but he did agree with the scriptures that define God as our loving Father. He did not ask his followers to follow the gods of the Christian creeds but only the God spoken of in scripture.

A prophet will have dreams and visions from God (see Numbers 12:6). When Jacob was running away from his brother Esau, he saw a vision of angels ascending to and descending from heaven in a dream. Jacob became a prophet of God. God spoke to Moses from a burning bush, and Moses became a prophet. Peter fell into a trance and saw a vision in which he was told that what God had cleansed he was not to call unclean. Peter learned that the gospel was for gentiles as well as Jews. Peter was a prophet.

Joseph Smith had a vision when he was fourteen years old. He saw God the Father and Jesus Christ in that vision. About three years later, he saw an angel named Moroni, who told him of the Book of Mormon. He, like Paul, saw into heaven and wrote some of what he saw there (see D&C 76). Joseph F. Smith, Joseph Smith's nephew and a later prophet in the Church, saw the world of spirits and what is going on there (D&C 138). My great-grandmother saw, in a dream, two missionaries of the Church coming to teach her the gospel so she would be ready to receive them. I have seen—in a night vision—the spirit world, so I could be more faithful in doing the work to help those people there. Joseph and his followers have dreams and visions just as the prophets in the Bible did. They meet these criteria for being prophets.

How to Recognize False Prophets

This is very easy. If someone says something will happen and it doesn't, you can know he is a false prophet (see Deuteronomy 18:22). Noah predicted the flood, but only his family listened to him. It happened. Isaiah and Jeremiah predicted the captivity of the Jews, but the

Jews did not listen. They were taken to Babylon as slaves. Christ predicted his own death and Resurrection. His disciples did not believe him until they saw it with their own eyes. Doubting Thomas had to see to believe. Oh, we of little faith.

In our own day, there have been many that have predicted the coming of Christ and the end of the world. The time was set for Christ's coming and they waited for him, but he never showed up. When one prophecy failed, they just made another prediction for a few years later and waited patiently for the "Rapture." It has not yet happened. It seems like after a few times of getting it wrong, the people would stop believing these false prophets.

Now let us consider Joseph Smith. Did he ever make predictions that happened? The second section of this book makes it plain that his prophecies were fulfilled. He wrote of the Civil War thirty years before it happened, even specifying where it would start and what it eventually would be about. He predicted that the Saints would eventually go to the Rocky Mountains and there become a great people. The Saints ended up in the Rocky Mountains as he said, but only because the people of the United States drove them out of their homes and left them no other choice. His predictions or revelations have happened, sometimes without his followers even trying to make them happen.

Some have said it was a false prophecy when Joseph said the Saints would settle in Jackson and its surrounding counties in Missouri. The Saints were driven by mobs out of Missouri and Illinois and they finally settled in the Salt Lake Valley of Utah. If we compare this with the Prophet Jonah, however, we find a similarity. Jonah went to the people of Nineveh and prophesied their destruction if they did not repent. The people repented, and their city was saved. Jonah, however, became miffed at the Lord when the city was not destroyed at the set time. Jonah thought his prophecy should be fulfilled. The Lord had changed his mind because the people had repented. It is the same with Jackson County, Missouri, only here the people did not repent enough. Because they did not repent and follow the commandments as a group, they were not allowed to stay in Missouri. Since they were his people in Zion, the Lord expected even more of them than he did the other members of the Church. Of course, there is still time for the Saints to go to Missouri. This prophecy may yet be fulfilled. Be patient. There is land there for you to buy if you want to go there. The extermination order of Governor Boggs has been rescinded, so you need not fear for your life.

Joseph Smith meets the test of a prophet. He was called by God, served God as God wanted to be served, witnessed of Christ, published new scripture, had dreams and visions, and made predictions that have come true.

About the Author

Dale Spears was born on June 2, 1954 in White County, Tennessee. His father was a farmer and his mother worked in a shirt factory to provide some spending money. His elementary school was a little two-room school house with grades one through four in one room and five through eight in the other. His father joined the LDS Church in 1919 and his mother converted not long after she married, so Dale was raised in the gospel. However, at that time, there was no meetinghouse for Church meetings unless the missionaries borrowed one from one of the other churches. As a local missionary, Dale's father held cottage meetings with the few members that were around.

Dale served a mission in the California Arcadia Mission. It was a bit of a change for a country boy from Tennessee to be put into East Los Angeles, and Dale certainly experienced some culture shock. After his mission, Dale attended BYU and eventually graduated, though it took a little longer than usual because he chose to work his way through school, earning the money first and then taking classes. He also got a teaching certificate for middle school and high school and learned American Sign Language, square dancing, and some karate on the side.

After school, Dale got a job as an American Sign Language interpreter in the public school system. After a few years, he went into special education and stayed there for the next twenty years. While he enjoyed teaching, Dale has found writing even more stimulating. From a young age, he has studied the gospel in depth and now hopes to share some of his findings with others.